Productivity Assessment in Education

Anita A. Summers, *Editor*

NEW DIRECTIONS FOR TESTING AND MEASUREMENT
MICHAEL KEAN, *Editor-in-Chief*

Number 15, September 1982

Paperback sourcebooks in
The Jossey-Bass Social and Behavioral Sciences Series

Jossey-Bass Inc., Publishers
San Francisco • Washington • London

Productivity Assessment in Education
Number 15, September 1982
    Anita A. Summers, *Editor*

New Directions for Testing and Measurement Series
Michael Kean, *Editor-in-Chief*

New Directions for Testing and Measurement is published
quarterly by Jossey-Bass Inc., Publishers. Subscriptions, single-issue
orders, change of address notices, undelivered copies, and other
correspondence should be sent to *New Directions* Subscriptions,
Jossey-Bass Inc., Publishers, 433 California Street, San Francisco,
California 94104.

Editorial correspondence should be sent to the Editor-in-Chief,
Michael Kean, ETS, Evanston, Illinois 60201.

Library of Congress Catalogue Card Number LC 81-48588
International Standard Serial Number ISSN 0271-0609
International Standard Book Number ISBN 87589-929-3

Cover art by Willi Baum
Manufactured in the United States of America

Ordering Information

The paperback sourcebooks listed below are published quarterly and can be ordered either by subscription or as single copies.

Subscriptions cost $35.00 per year for institutions, agencies, and libraries. Individuals can subscribe at the special rate of $21.00 per year *if payment is by personal check.* (Note that the full rate of $35.00 applies if payment is by institutional check, even if the subscription is designated for an individual.) Standing orders are accepted.

Single copies are available at $7.95 when payment accompanies order, and *all single-copy orders under $25.00 must include payment.* (California, Washington, D.C., New Jersey, and New York residents please include appropriate sales tax.) For billed orders, cost per copy is $7.95 plus postage and handling. (Prices subject to change without notice.)

To ensure correct and prompt delivery, all orders must give either the *name of an individual* or an *official purchase order number.* Please submit your order as follows:

Subscriptions: specify series and subscription year.
Single Copies: specify sourcebook code and issue number (such as, TM8).

Mail orders for United States and Possessions, Latin America, Canada, Japan, Australia, and New Zealand to:
Jossey-Bass Inc., Publishers
433 California Street
San Francisco, California 94104

Mail orders for all other parts of the world to:
Jossey-Bass Limited
28 Banner Street
London EC1Y 8QE

New Directions for Testing and Measurement Series
Michael Kean, *Editor-in-Chief*

Contents

Editor's Notes

During the last twenty-five years, economists have begun to look into many issues of public policy that previously were regarded as the exclusive province of such professions as sociology, education, and law. Econometric techniques and economic theory, formerly used to address only such problems as unemployment, profit maximization, and tax incidence, have been employed to explore the problems of crime, health, and educational achievement. In this volume, the current state of this exploration is examined in the area of educational productivity. As a reading of its chapters will reveal, the report card on the usefulness of economic methods is not uniform. Relatively low grades are given by the authors of the first two chapters, and relatively high grades are given by the authors of the last four chapters. Each chapter, of course, examines the work from a different perspective.

Richard Murnane reviews the literature on education production functions, beginning with the seminal work of James Coleman, and concludes that it has established that the characteristics of teachers and students dominate the impact of other school inputs on learning. But, he argues, we are limited in our ability to draw policy recommendations from this research for three reasons. First, teachers and students are assigned nonrandomly, so that it is difficult to separate input effectiveness from influence assignment. Second, the attributes of teachers and students are bundled and cannot be separated perfectly with available data and statistical procedures. Third, any change in resource allocation will set in motion new responses that may alter the predicted result. Murnane argues that greatly increased exchange between educational researchers and educational practitioners will do much to reduce the hazards attendant on translating research into policy.

David Long and Sandra McMullan are attorneys who have been active in many school finance reform cases. They examine the usefulness of educational productivity research in such litigation. They demonstrate that plaintiffs generally concern themselves with equal allocation of educational resources, not with effectiveness. Defendants have drawn upon input-output research to argue that differences in resources do not translate into differences in achievement changes, but plaintiffs have argued that the limitations of the research make it unsatisfactory as a policy guide. The courts, on the whole, have not drawn upon the research on educational productivity to pronounce on the constitutionality of educational systems. Instead, they have focused on allocation of inputs, not on how allocation affects output.

In short, the first two chapters suggest that there are many limitations on the translation of educational productivity analysis into policy. Some limitations are inherent; others can be minimized. Clearly, however, one major institution, the courts, regards these limitations as significant enough to justify putting the research findings aside. The last four chapters take a different tack. Their authors argue that the problems can be reduced, and as a result they are relatively optimistic about the usefulness of input-output analyses. Their optimism stems both from their attack on the limitations and from their pragmatic concern for the current acute need for improved educational efficiency — more output for the same inputs, or the same output from fewer inputs.

In Chapter Three, Mark Raivetz and I address several concerns raised by educational productivity research, using samples from the Philadelphia School District. The data on pupils are specific to the pupil. Detailed data on how reading programs were delivered in the classroom were available, as was a good deal of data on the behavior and attitudes of teachers and principals. School admininstrators, reading specialists, and union representatives were consulted as part of the study. Two samples of students were drawn. One was used to refine the hypotheses; the other, to test them. We concluded, first, that the findings were robust enough to warrant recommending some reallocation of resources and, second, that it would be useful for schools to use this type of evaluation on a regular basis.

In the next chapter, Susan Cochrane and Dean Jamison of the World Bank demonstrate how extensions of the traditional educational production function analysis give insight into the spread of education that always characterizes modernization in developing nations. They use rural Thailand as a case study to examine the factors affecting educational attainment — defined here as years of schooling completed — and participation. They examine data on three generations and conclude that age and innate ability determine participation in school for those between the ages of fourteen and twenty-five, not landownership, younger children in the family, or child employment in the village. For girls, even in this society, which has a high degree of equity in education, the mother's desire for her daughter's education also plays a important role. For younger children and older boys, access to school is an important determinant of attainment. The authors regard these conclusions as suggestive for other developing nations.

In Chapter Five, Barbara Wolfe and Jere Behrman explore data on education from Nicaragua and reach results that extend the impact areas of education beyond the conventional ones. They look at the effects on paid labor market activity (earnings, labor force participation), household production (child mortality and health, nutrient intake, contraceptive knowledge), and other factors (fertility, use of contraceptives, migration). The high productivity expected of education, which underlies the estimated $40 billion spent annually in the developing countries on that function, poses a problem far more complex than the research generally recognizes. Wolfe and Behrman argue that the factors that are usually omitted from such calculations result in overstatements of productivity in some instances (reduction in nonmarket activities, for example) and in underestimates of productivity in others (increase in health and nutrition as a result of schooling, for example). Their findings propose a new agenda for future work.

In the final chapter, Stephen Mullin, with full recognition of the limitations and difficulties of educational production functions, argues vigorously for a review of its use as a resource allocation tool. The tightening of public budgets makes this tool essential to rational decision making, since the only alternative is nonselective constraints, such as capping legislation. In Mullin's view, preoccupation with equity issues during the 1960s and 1970s caused efficiency considerations to be overlooked. Now, fiscal pressures, increased judicial concern for efficiency, and improvements in research techniques all suggest that redesign of educational finance reform strategies is desirable. Mullin argues that such redesign must relate output measures to students, emphasize cost-effectiveness, the equity to output measures, and develop an equalizing formula that incorporates efficiency incentives.

What can we conclude about the state of the art of educational productivity measurement from these six chapters? To me, these chapters indicate that recent advances in the measurement of relevant inputs have been substantial and that incorporation of some aspects of the economic models has broadened our understanding of the role of education. The question is, Are these advances being incorporated into policy? At the present time, the courts do not appear to be very interested in these recent developments. However, public fiscal pressures and increased exchanges between educational researchers and practitioners give us grounds for optimism that other institutions — legislatures and school boards — will be interested. The authors hope that this sourcebook will contribute to that dialogue.

Anita A. Summers
Editor

Anita A. Summers is professor and associate chairperson of public management in the Wharton School of the University of Pennsylvania.

Input-output research has made valuable contributions to our understanding of schools; however, it does not provide reliable evidence concerning how school resources should be allocated.

Input-Output Research in Education: Accomplishments, Limitations, and Lessons

Richard J. Murnane

In the last sixteen years, quantitative research on school effectiveness — called educational production function studies by economists, input-output studies by sociologists, and research on the cost-quality issue by lawyers — has played a significant role in public policy debates concerning a range of educational issues. The results of school effectiveness studies have been introduced into court cases dealing with the way in which schools are financed, into legislative debates concerning compensatory education, and into deliberations of the executive branch concerning school busing.

The prominent role that this research has played in policy discussions has led many observers to ask: How good is the research? What does it really have to tell us? Does it provide reliable evidence concerning the allocation of scarce resources? The purpose of this chapter is to address these questions. One of the lessons of the analysis that will be conducted here — the importance of talking to school people about alternative explanations for empirical findings — has potential for increasing dialogue between researchers and school officials and for throwing light on the actual school policies that influence student achievement.

A. Summers (Ed.). *New Directions for Testing and Measurement: Productivity Assessment in Education*, no. 15. San Francisco: Jossey-Bass, September 1982.

6

Accomplishments

In the sixteen years since the publication of *Equality of Educational Opportunity* (Coleman and others, 1966), the first large-scale quantitative study of school effectiveness, important advances have been made in the methodology used to study the relationship of school resources to student achievement. These advances include the use of longitudinal data to measure student gains in skills from one school year to the next and the use of more accurate measures of the school resources actually available to individual students. As a result of these methodological advances, quantitative studies of school effectiveness, which I will refer to as input-output studies, can now provide quite detailed descriptions of relationships that exist between school resources and student achievement over the course of a school year.

What have these descriptions revealed? The most important finding is that there are significant differences in the amount of learning that takes place in different schools and in different classrooms within the same school, even among inner-city schools and even after taking into account the skills and backgrounds that children bring to school (Armor and others, 1976; Hanushek, 1971; Murnane, 1975). Until the late 1960s, few policy makers would have found this result interesting. Like most Americans, policy makers believed that schooling mattered and recognized that they and their children learned more in some years of formal schooling than in other years. However, in recent years, frustration resulting both from difficulties in finding policy levers to improve schools and from disappointing evaluations of policy innovations that were actually carried out has shaken this confidence. The results indicating clear differences among schools and classrooms affirm that it is worthwhile to devote attention to the fact that some schools provide better education than other schools do, although our success in tracing this fact to the policies responsible for it has been limited.

The second important set of positive findings from the quantitative research on school effectiveness points to the critical importance of the schools' human resources — teachers and students. Due to data limitations, large-scale input-output studies have yet to investigate the role of the school principal. However, school effectiveness studies using other kinds of research designs (Edmonds, 1979) indicate that school principals play a central role in determining school effectiveness.

Virtually all studies find that some attributes of teachers are significantly related to student achievement. The attributes most commonly related to student achievement involve teachers' intellectual skills, as indicated by scores on tests of verbal ability or the quality of the college that the teacher attended (Hanushek, 1979, 1981; Murnane, 1981; Summers and Wolfe, 1977; Winkler, 1975).

Many studies also report the importance of student body composition. While the results vary somewhat across studies, there is support for the hypothesis that elementary school children with low initial skill levels who attend schools in which their classmates' average achievement level is relatively high make more progress than similar children who attend schools in which their classmate's average achievement level is relatively low. There is similar evidence regarding socioeconomic status (Henderson, Mieszkowski, and Sauvageau, 1978; Summers and Wolfe, 1977; Winkler, 1975).

To appreciate the contribution of recent input-output research to our understanding of schools, it will be helpful to place this research in a historical perspective. Quantitative research on school effectiveness began with a broadly specified model that was agnostic on the roles played by particular school resources. In this model, a large number of resources were treated in parallel fashion, including physical facilities, such as the number of library books and the size and age of the school, as well as human resources. We now understand that the primary resources are teachers and students. If other resources matter, it is through their impact on the behaviors of teachers and students.

Limitations

While there has been growing agreement among researchers and policy makers concerning the school resources that are most important (Hanushek, 1979; Murnane, 1981), there is no such agreement concerning the policy implications of these findings. Some economists have suggested that the results indicate how school resources should be allocated, and they have formalized this suggestion by incorporating the results of input-output studies into optimizing algorithms designed to show how school districts should allocate resources to reach particular goals (Boardman, 1978; Cohn, 1980). Other economists, while not stating what school officials should do with dollars, argue that schools must presently be using resources inefficiently, since the pattern of payments of resources does not reflect the relative values of the regression coefficients in input-output studies (Hanushek, 1981).

Many school officials view these interpretations of the evidence with skepticism. They feel intuitively that the quantitative research does not capture all the information needed for good policy making. Moreover, while school officials sometimes concede that resources could be used more effectively, most believe that dollars as currently used are related to school quality. However, since few school officials are trained researchers, most are unable to express the sources of their skepticism in the language of models and statistics. At the same time, few researchers have tried to elicit from school officials ideas about aspects of schooling that should be reflected in the design of quantitative research. Thus, as a result of differences in training and inclinations, little dialogue takes place between quantitative researchers and school officials.

In the following paragraphs, I explain the methodological limitations of input-output research in education that I believe to underlie the skepticism of school officials. These limitations make it inappropriate to base decisions about the allocation of school resources on the results of such research.

Input-Output Data as Snapshots. Input-output research essentially provides snapshots — albeit increasingly fine-grained snapshots — of relationships between school resources and student achievement. To serve as an adequate basis for resource allocation decisions, these snapshots must fulfill two conditions: First, they must provide accurate information about the (unobserved) school process; second, they must accurately predict how that process would be altered and how student achievement would be affected by changes in allocations of school resources. It is my contention that input-output research in education does not fulfill these conditions; thus, it cannot tell us how to allocate school resources. To clarify my reasons for taking this position, it is useful to contrast input-output research in education with similar research in agriculture.

In an oft-cited paper, Heady (1957) reported on his investigations of the optimal combinations of fertilizers — nitrogen and phosphate — that farmers use in growing corn. Heady began his research by conducting controlled experiments to determine the effects of different input levels of the fertilizers on corn yields. He then analyzed his experimental data with multivariate methods to estimate the input-output relationships between fertilizer combinations and corn yield. Finally, Heady incorporated information on the prices of the two inputs with the results of the input-output study to calculate how farmers should combine inputs of nitrogen and phosphate to maximize the yield from a given level of expenditures on fertilizer. Three characteristics of Heady's research allowed his results to serve as a reasonably reliable policy guide for farmers. First, Heady used controlled experiments to assure that his results did in fact reflect the causal influences of the fertilizers on corn yields. Second, the inputs were well-defined homogenous commodities available in well-operating markets at clearly identified prices. Third, the input mix could be changed simply by altering the amounts of nitrogen and phosphate that were purchased and then spread on the corn fields.

Contrast the characteristics of Heady's research with the situation facing the researcher investigating input-output relations in education. First, education researchers must rely on data from natural experiments — that is, from the variations in resource combinations that naturally occur in schools. This significantly limits the researcher's ability to assess causation, not only because the critical school resources — teachers and students — are not assigned to each other by a random assignment process, but also because a variety of formal and informal assignment procedures in fact tend to group students with particular characteristics. As a result, it is extremely difficult to disentangle input-output relationships from the influence of assignment procedures.

Second, in input-output research in education, the critical resources — teachers and students — are characterized by their attributes (for example, race, sex, experience, and education of teachers and socioeconomic backgrounds and prior skill levels of students). However, it is not possible for schools to acquire individual attributes, only bundles of correlated attributes. Moreover, the bundles cannot be purchased in well-defined markets at clearly defined prices. Instead, the acquisition process is restricted to the establishment of personnel policies and student attendance policies, to which teachers and students respond.

Third, changing the resource allocation mix — that is, the combinations of teachers and students that work together — requires changing personnel policies, student attendance policies, or both. These changes often elicit responses from teachers and students that are unpredicted. Responses to certain busing programs (Rissell and Hawley, 1981) and teacher layoff programs (Johnson, 1980) are cases in point. Input-output research as it is currently conducted, does not examine the nature of these responses, because it takes as given the combination of teachers and students present in different classrooms and different schools. Consequently, the resource allocation process is beyond the observation and control of the analyst.

As a result of their experiences and frustrations in trying to create effective school programs, school officials are aware at least implicitly of some of the factors that so powerfully differentiate the utility of input-output research in education from its utility in agriculture. In particular, they know that it is difficult to change personnel and student attendance policies, and they know that policy changes often elicit responses very different from the responses expected. It is this knowledge that produces the skepticism of many school officials concerning the policy implications of input-output studies.

Many research puzzles reflect the difficulty of capturing critical elements of the process of schooling with input-output research. However, the examples that follow show how altering the research design to reflect the intuitions and observations of school officials can diminish the puzzling nature of results and increase the extent to which research provides insights into the ways that the actions of teachers and students affect student achievement.

Teacher Experience. The relationship between teaching experience and teaching effectiveness is one of the most heavily researched questions in education. However, despite many studies, the evidence remains inconclusive. Some studies report positive relationships between teaching experience and teaching performance, as measured by student achievement gains (Hanushek, 1972; Kean and others, 1979; Kiesling, 1981). One study reports a negative relationship between teacher experience and effectiveness in teaching students with certain characteristics (Summers and Wolfe, 1977). Many other studies report no significant relationship between teaching experience and performance (Armor and others, 1976; Hanushek, 1981; Henderson, Mieszkowski, and Sauvageau, 1978; Link and Ratledge, 1979). Many school officials find these results puzzling. From their observations of individual teachers over time, they conclude that most teachers learn a great deal about how to teach in their first years on the job and that such learning by doing results in improved teaching.

In fact, the puzzling and conflicting nature of research findings is due at least in part to the research methodology used to study the relationship between experience and performance. To date, input-output studies have not investigated the impact of learning by doing on teaching performance by the most reliable method, namely, by examining how the performance of individual teachers changes as they acquire experience. Instead, the studies have investigated the relationship between experience and performance for a sample of teachers at one point in time. Implicitly, these studies assume that, after observable differences among teachers (such as the quality of the college that they attended) are taken in account, the only other reasons why teachers should differ in effectiveness results from differences in their learning by doing. However, there may be important unobserved differences in the effectiveness of teachers hired in different years that are not the result of learning by doing. These differences are the result of vintage effects and self-selection effects.

Vintage Effects. Vintage effects are differences in the average abilities of teachers hired by school districts at different times—for example, in different years. The most compelling explanation for the existence of vintage effects is that dramatic changes in labor market conditions for teachers over the last twenty-five years have affected the quality of new entrants to the teaching profession. In the late 1950s and early 1960s, a rapid increase in student enrollments created an acute shortage of teachers in the United States. Many school districts, particularly urban districts, found it difficult to find qualified applicants to fill vacant positions. By 1970, this situation had changed significantly. A decrease in the demand for teachers (precipitated by declining enrollments) combined with an increase in the supply of teachers (a delayed response to the earlier shortage) to produce a surplus of teachers that has persisted in most subject areas since 1970. As a result, school districts have been able to be very selective in choosing among the large number of applicants for individual teaching positions. If we can assume that district personnel officers are able to identify applicants with the greatest potential, the average quality of new teachers should be higher in periods of excess supply than in periods of excess demand. Unless the differences in the average abilities of teachers hired at different times are captured by variables describing teaching backgrounds—and this is very difficult to do — research based on a cross section of teachers cannot produce reliable estimates of the influence of teaching experience on teaching performance.

In an attempt to improve the methodology used to estimate the impact of experience on teaching performance, Murnane and Phillips (1981) constructed an explicit measure of vintage effects for a sample of teachers in one large urban school district to investigate the sensitivity of estimates of the relationship between experience and performance to the inclusion of that measure. The measure of vintage effects consisted of the change in total student enrollment in the school district between the year in which the teacher first taught in the district and the previous year. The logic underlying use of this measure was that, in years of rapidly growing student enrollment, this and neighboring districts, which were all competing for teachers in the same labor market, hired large numbers of teachers at a time when the supply of teachers was relatively limited. As a result, districts could not be selective in choosing among applicants. However, when enrollments were on the decline, personnel officers could be more selective, and average teacher quality would rise.

The variable included in the model to indicate learning by doing was the natural logarithm of each teacher's total number of years of teaching experience. This specification reflected the assumption that teachers continue to learn as they gain experience but that the greatest gains from additional experience occur in the first years of teaching.

The empirical results indicated that teaching experience was not significantly related to teaching performance when vintage effects were not taken into account. However, when vintage effects were taken into account, teaching experience was positively related to teaching performance. The size of the relevant coefficient implied that children taught by a teacher with five years of experience made three to four more months of progress in acquiring reading skills during a school year than did children taught by a first-year teacher.

The key lesson of this investigation is that teachers' career decisions, which are made in the context of changing labor market conditions, make it extremely difficult to use cross sectional data to capture one important element of the schooling process — namely, how the performance of teachers changes as they gain experience.

Self-Selection Effects. Self-selection is another explanation for the puzzling results of cross sectional research on the relationship between teaching experience and teaching performance. The self-selection hypothesis states that the effectiveness of teachers who choose to remain in the profession (or in a particular school district) may differ systematically from the effectiveness of teachers who choose to leave. For example, it may be only the most able teachers who survive the difficult first years of teaching. Conversely, effective, experienced teachers may leave the classroom to become administrators. Or, effective teachers may be the most likely to leave teaching to pursue occupations in which high skill levels are rewarded with especially high salaries. Self-selection effects, like vintage effects, confound attempts to use cross sectional data on teachers to assess the impact of learning by doing on teaching performance.

Class Size. The relationship between class size and student achievement has been another confusing issue in educational research. Despite the efforts of much research and the use of increasingly large and data sets, no consensus has been reached on the role that class size plays in determining student achievement. Many educators are skeptical about the inconclusive research findings, because their experiences suggest that most teachers do a better job in helping children to learn when they do not need to spread their efforts over a large number of children.

As in the case of the relationship between experience and performance, one reason for the ambiguous research results involves the difficulty of capturing critical aspects of the process of schooling with essentially snapshot research. In the case of class size research, this difficulty is reflected in confusion about the appropriate definition of the concept. Should class size refer to the number of children in the class on any given day, or should it refer to the number of different children whom a teacher must serve during a given school year? In schools in which there is no turnover among students, there is no difference between these two definitions. However, as the principal of one urban elementary school explained to me, in schools that serve highly mobile student populations, the number of children in a class on any given day may be much smaller than the total number of students whom the teacher serves during the school year. In such schools, teachers are continually faced with the problem of integrating new children into the class. This task imposes large demands on teacher time and reduces the time available for instruction. Consequently, in classes in which there is a significant amount of student turnover, the number of students in the class at any one time does not always reflect the demands of instruction received by students who stay in the class for the entire year.

Thus, in effect, there are two alternative dimensions of class size: the average number of students in the classroom on any given day, and the total number of different students who belong to the class during the school year. Holding average class size constant, the total number of students will increase as student turnover increases. Both dimensions of class size can have an impact on student achievement.

Using information from a sample of 800 inner-city elementary school children and their teachers, Murnane (1975) examined the impact on student achievement of these two dimensions of class size. Average class size was measured by the average of the number of students enrolled in a given class on October 15 and on April 15. The total number of students served was measured by the total number of names that appeared on the class register for the school year. The results indicated that average class size was not significantly related to student achievement. This may have been due to the limited variation in average class size in the sample. However, the total number of students who passed through the class, which varied from one more than average class size to twenty-two more than average class size, was negatively related to student achievement.

The primary lesson from this investigation is similar to the lesson of the preceding example, namely, that the active behaviors of human resources make it difficult to capture critical elements of the schooling process with cross sectional data. In this case, students' mobility made average class size a poor measure of the demands on teachers' time and confounded attempts to investigate whether the level of these demands affected student achievement.

Lessons

One lesson to be drawn from the two input-output studies just described is that the intuitions of experienced school officials should be heeded by researchers when designing input-output research. Often, school officials' perceptions of what affects student achievement in their schools can be incorporated into input-output research, where it will improve the ability of the research to capture critical dimensions of the ways in which schooling affects students' achievement. For example, in the experience and class size studies, just described, interviews with school officials produced the ideas for studying vintage effects and student turnover.

A second lesson is that it is important to consider a broad set of possible interpretations of coefficients in input-output studies. In other words, researchers should think carefully about alternative explanations of significant coefficients and view as highly plausible — and also potentially interesting — explanations other than the usual explanations that the relevant right-hand side variable had a causal influence on student achievement.

The reason why alternative explanations can be highly plausible is that the resource combinations present in particular classrooms are determined by the large number of personnel and student assignment policies, explicit and implicit, present in all school districts and by the reactions of students and teachers to these policies. Policies and the reactions of human resources to them influence student achievement in many different and often unpredictable ways. These influences often result in significant coefficients in input-output studies, but often they do not reflect causal relationships between the observed explanatory variables and student achievement.

Careful researchers do try to be sensitive to these alternative explanations, and many published articles describing the results of input-output studies contain footnotes that mention alternative explanations for particular significant coefficients. However, relegation of these alternative explanations to footnotes suggests that most researchers view them as problems obstructing the estimation of the central input-output relationship, not as interesting and potentially important phenomena in their own right.

The language used in the econometric literature to describe such alternative explanations—selectivity bias, omitted variables, nonrandom samples—reflects the same perspective. Such terms connote problems that obstruct researchers' attempts to examine a particular well-defined concept, such as an input-output relationship. In cases like the fertilizer–corn yield example (in which the input-output relationship is clearly defined, independent of resource allocation mechanisms, and still a critical puzzle), this perspective is reasonable. It keeps the researcher focused on the one central question. In the fertilizer–corn yield case, it was both possible and appropriate to focus exclusively on the input-output relationship. Moreover, the same focus could answer the policy question of what to do with scarce resources, because buying and allocating the relevant inputs involved no significant puzzles or process difficulties.

The education case is quite different, however. The critical resources—teachers and students—simply cannot be purchased and placed in classrooms. Instead, changes in human resource combinations can only be brought about by changing personnel or student attendance policies. Often, the intended changes in resource combinations do not occur, because teachers, students, or both respond to the policy changes in unpredicted ways. In other words, teachers' and students' reactions to the many formal and informal rules and policies that characterize schools are aspects of the schooling process that are not well understood, although they are critical in determining how schools influence students. Pursuing alternative explanations of puzzling results of input-output studies is one potentially fruitful way of learning more about these poorly understood aspects.

To illustrate this suggestion, consider two examples of findings from recent input-output studies that are somewhat puzzling and that have many alternative explanations: Murnane (1975) found that black teachers in an urban school system were more effective in teaching reading skills to black primary school children than white teachers in the school system were. Among the conventional explanations for this finding that are consistent with a causal interpretation are that black teachers understand the needs and motivational patterns of black students better than white teachers do and that black teachers provide a role model that inspires black students to greater effort. However, explanations of a somewhat different nature are also possible. For example, most of the black teachers in the sample had been educated at one of a small number of black colleges in the South. Personal connections with placement officers in these colleges might have enabled the school district personnel director to recruit the most able graduates of these schools. Another possibility is that differential alternative employment possibilities made it less likely for talented black teachers to leave the school system after a few years of teaching than they did for talented white teachers. Both explanations concern idiosyncratic aspects of the operation of labor markets that are important to understand in designing policies to recruit and retain talented teachers. Interviewing the personnel director and the relevant black teachers might have provided information about the relevance of these alternative explanations.

A second example concerns Summers and Wolfe's (1977) counterintuitive finding that, for students who began the school year with an average or below-average achievement level, the number of disruptive incidents that occurred during the school year was positively associated with growth in student achievement. To the authors' credit, the disruptions variable was not deleted from the analysis, and one possible explanation of the finding was discussed in their text—namely, that the results might stem from the aggregated nature of the disruption data. However, it also seems reasonable to ask whether alternative explanations could go beyond simple artifacts of data limitations to reflect real things going on in schools. At least two possibilities occur to this writer: First, that in such schools only atypical students take achievement tests (a necessary condition for inclusion in the sample); second, that administrators have found ways of attracting particularly effective teachers to troubled schools.

Undoubtedly, there are a variety of other possible explanations. However, the point of this discussion is not to defend any particular explanation. Instead, the point is to argue that diligent exploration of a variety of possible explanations for puzzling results can uncover intended or unintended aspects of the schooling process that are important in determining students' achievement.

This type of research requires methods, such as interviews of school officials, with which researchers who specialize in quantitative analysis generally are not comfortable. However, to conduct interviews with the explicit objective of unraveling puzzles posed by the results of quantitative research could greatly enhance the contributions of quantitative research to determinations of the important elements of the schooling process and ultimately provide information that could lead to better schools.

References

Armor, D., and others. *Analysis of the School Preferred Reading Program in Selected Los Angeles Minority Schools.* Santa Monica, Calif.: Rand, 1976.

Boardman, A. E. "Policy Models for the Management of Student Achievement and Other Educational Outputs." *Management Science,* 1978, *8,* 99–122.

Cohn, E. "Combining Efficiency and Equity: Optimization of Resource Allocation in State School Systems." In W. W. McMahon and T. G. Geske (Eds.), *Toward Efficiency and Equity in Educational Finance.* Boston: Allyn & Bacon, 1980.

16

Coleman, J. S., and others. *Equality of Educational Opportunity.* Washington, D. C.: Office of Education, National Center for Education Statistics, 1966.

Edmonds, R. R. "Some Schools Work and More Can." *Social Policy,* 1979, *9* (5), 28–32.

Hanushek, E. A. "Teacher Characteristics and Gains in Student Achievement: Estimation Using Micro Data." *American Economic Review,* 1971, *61,* 280–288.

Hanushek, E. A. *Education and Race.* Lexington, Mass.: Heath, 1972.

Hanushek, E. A. "Conceptual and Empirical Issues in the Estimation of Educational Production Functions." *Journal of Human Resources,* 1979, *14,* 351–388.

Hanushek, E. A. "Throwing Money at Schools." *Journal of Policy Analysis and Management,* 1981, *1* (1), 19–41.

Heady, E. O. "An Econometric Investigation of the Technology of Agricultural Production Functions." *Econometrica,* 1957, *25,* 249–268.

Henderson, V., Mieszkowski, P., and Sauvageau, T. "Peer-Group Effects and Educational Production Functions." *Journal of Public Economics,* 1978, *10,* 97–106.

Johnson, S. M. "Performance-Based Staff Layoffs in the Public Schools: Implementation and Outcomes." *Harvard Educational Review,* 1980, *50,* 214–233.

Kean, M. H., Summers, A. A., Raivetz, M. J., and Farber, I. J. *What Works in Reading?* Philadelphia: Office of Research and Evaluation, School District of Philadelphia, 1979.

Kiesling, J. "The Production of Reading." Indiana University, mimeo, 1981.

Link, C. R., and Ratledge, E. C. "Student Perceptions, IQ, and Achievement." *The Journal of Human Resources,* 1979, *14* (1), 98–111.

Murnane, R. J. *The Impact of School Resources on the Learning of Inner-City Children.* Cambridge, Mass.: Ballinger, 1975.

Murnane, R. J. "Interpreting the Evidence of School Effectiveness." *Teachers College Record,* 1981, *83* (1), 19–35.

Murnane, R. J., and Phillips, B. "Learning by Doing, Vintage, and Selection: Three Pieces of the Puzzle Relating Teaching Experience and Teaching Performance." *Economics of Education Review,* 1981, *1* (4), 453–465.

Rissell, C., and Hawley, W. "Understanding White Flight and Doing Something About It." In W. Hawley (Ed.), *Effective School Desegregation.* Beverly Hills, Calif.: Sage, 1981.

Summers, A. A., and Wolfe, B. L. "Do Schools Make a Difference?" *American Economic Review,* 1977, *67* (4), 639–652.

Winkler, D. R. "Educational Achievement and School Peer-Group Composition." *The Journal of Human Resources,* 1975, *10,* 189–204.

Richard J. Murnane is assistant professor of economics at Yale University. His research interests include teacher labor markets, the effects of school and home environments on children's achievement, and regulation of human services industries.

Although educational productivity research has been much debated
in school finance litigation, it has proved largely irrelevant to resolution
by the courts of broad equity issues raised by the allocation of educational
resources among school districts.

Educational Productivity Issues in School Finance Litigation

David C. Long
Sandra H. McMullan

For more than a decade, courts throughout the nation have had to resolve legal challenges to statewide school financing systems that, it is claimed, discriminate against children in poor school districts. Such discrimination has taken the form of unequal expenditures and educational inputs among school districts. Typically, this inequality has been caused by the disparate property tax bases of school districts in educational finance systems that rely heavily on local property tax revenues. Plaintiffs in such cases have shown that inequities in educational expenditures translate into inequalities in educational inputs — staff, programs and services, materials, equipment, and facilities.

In response, defendants have argued that research on educational productivity is ambiguous about the relationship between differences in levels and types of educational resources and differences in educational outcomes among students, when the latter are measured primarily by scores on standardized achievement tests; thus, inequalities in educational expenditures and inputs are inconsequential for children. Plaintiffs, in turn, have responded that, while the state cannot ensure particular educational outcomes, it should not be

A. Summers (Ed.). *New Directions for Testing and Measurement: Productivity Assessment in Education*, no. 15.
San Francisco: Jossey-Bass, September 1982.

permitted to discriminate among children in the provision of educational opportunities as measured by educational resources and that any agnosticism among educational researchers about input-output relationships provides no justification for allocating resources on the basis of criteria that have nothing to do with education, such as the size of a school district's tax base.

Despite the exchange of arguments in court, educational productivity issues have been of little consequence to courts faced with the question of whether school finance systems are unconstitutional. In general, courts have accepted educational inputs as the frame of reference when considering the fairness of state systems for allocation of educational resources, and they have applied traditional legal and equitable concepts of the relationship between the state and its citizens. Occasionally, educational achievement has been cited by courts as evidence that needy children are in low-wealth districts, but rarely has it been related to educational productivity.

In this chapter, we describe how the adversaries in school finance cases have dealt with educational productivity issues in the courtroom. Then, we review the courts' responses to these issues. Finally, we point to the possibility that educational productivity research can help to create fairer, constitutional school finance systems.

How Educational Productivity Issues Have Been Presented to the Courts

Plaintiffs' Presentation. For the most part, plaintiffs have not considered resolution of educational productivity issues to be relevant to their case. The issue for plaintiffs has been the unfairness of unequal allocation of revenues and expenditures and of the educational inputs that they purchase.

Plaintiffs in school finance cases have been children and parents representative of the class of children and parents in the school district that has been receiving unequal resources. In some cases, school districts themselves have been plaintiffs. Opposing them have been state education officials and other state officials who have been named as defendants representative of the interests of the state. In a few cases, wealthy school districts have intervened as defendants to protect their advantaged position under the status quo.

Educational productivity issues have not generally arisen during plaintiffs' initial case. Rather, plaintiffs' proof has focused on inequalities in expenditures and resources and the causes of these inequalities—particularly disparities among school districts in taxable valuation per pupil, from which local revenues for education must be generated. A major part of plaintiffs' case has been to show that inequalities in educational inputs resulted from inequalities in revenues and expenditures. The evidence that plaintiffs have marshaled to demonstrate educational input inequalities has included larger class sizes; fewer staff; less experienced and less well-trained staff; inability to attract staff from a competitive applicant pool and to retain experienced staff; inability to attract teachers in such areas as science, mathematics, and special education; fewer materials and supplies; fewer course offerings; inadequate maintenance; and unequal facilities. Other input inequalities have included diminished opportunities for children to become aware of their culture through experiences in art, music, and drama; nonexistent or reduced physical education programs; and nonexistent or reduced educational support services, such as counselors, nurses, clerical staff, and curriculum supervision. Differences have also surfaced in the availability of locally funded remedial programs at all levels; in the use of new teaching methods and instructional technologies, such as computers; and in fewer opportunities for in-service training.

Plaintiffs have also shown that children in wealthy, high-spending districts are no more educationally needy or deserving than children in poor, low-spending districts. In some cases, the contrast has been even more pointed, with plaintiffs demonstrating that poor, low-achieving children are concentrated in school districts that have the fewest resources.

Defendants' Presentation. In response, defendants—state officials and wealthy school districts—have contended that inequalities in expenditures and educational inputs are irrelevant unless plaintiffs can prove that they translate into diminished educational productivity for children in disadvantaged school districts, that children in districts with greater resources receive a measurable benefit from their greater resources in terms of educational outputs, or that increasing resources to plaintiff districts will measurably increase productivity.

Defendants have relied upon educational productivity research to show that the educational inputs that wealthier school districts have in greater abundance have not been demonstrated to produce significant achievement gains and that additional educational resources would not necessarily increase the achievement of students in poorer school districts. Defendants' witnesses—primarily economists and educational evaluators—have testified about the conflicting results of educational productivity research. Their major conclusion has been that few inputs have been shown consistently and unambiguously to have a significant marginal utility in producing increased achievement, when achievement is measured by scores on standardized achievement tests.

In early school finance cases, the testimony of defendants' expert witnesses focused primarily on such primitive input-output research as the Coleman Report. In recent cases, such testimony has also included more methodologically sophisticated studies, such as those conducted by Murnane and Summers and Wolfe. In some cases, defendants have had their experts analyze the relationship between school district inputs, such as expenditures per pupil, and average achievement test scores in the state in question. These analyses have been of low quality and virtual case studies of the methodological problems that have plagued educational productivity research. That is, they have been costly to prepare, they have enabled plaintiffs to demonstrate the limitations of such research, and they appear to have had little probative value.

Plaintiffs' Responses. Through the exchange of views between experts and the process of cross-examination, the full range of methodological flaws of educational productivity research has been canvassed. These flaws include the failure of educational productivity studies to use disaggregated data, the absence of longitudinal analysis, the absence of data on the treatments that specific children receive, the failure of standardized achievement tests to measure many of the objectives of schooling, and the lack of information on the impact of specific resources on different types of children. Plaintiffs have argued that the sole conclusion to be drawn from defendants' evidence is that educational productivity research is too primitive and flawed to serve as a policy guide for the allocation of educational resources.

Plaintiffs have also sought to show that the more recent and more rigorous input-output research, which has minimized some of the methodological problems of earlier studies, shows that certain educational inputs do in fact produce achievement gains and that certain inputs appear more important for some children, subject areas, and grade levels than others. Plaintiffs have not argued that elimination of irrational determinants of educational resources, such as the property wealth of school districts, will reduce the achievement gaps that exist, for example, between white and minority children and between children from affluent and low-income homes. Plaintiffs have conceded that an equitable distribution of educational resources does not necessarily ensure that all school districts will use them wisely and that the elimination of these inequalities does not eliminate the need for the state, its citizens, and educators to continue to address the issue of the wise use of resources, using whatever insights educational productivity research can provide in this regard.

Plaintiffs have also pointed out to the courts the irony of in-court arguments by state officials and wealthy school districts that, beyond some very minimal level, educational expenditures and resources make no difference. Plaintiffs have introduced into the record how, in other settings, state officials justify education budget requests to state legislators by the importance of the educational resources to be funded; how wealthy school districts point with pride to their superior resources and range of educational opportunities when justifying their budgets or seeking approval for voted levies; and how school and municipal officials are aware of the impact that the availability of a wide range of first-class educational inputs has on attracting parents interested in the education of their children to their communities. Defendants' inconsistency on the value of educational resources has not, however, prevented them from arguing that the level of educational resources makes little difference or that low-spending districts would simply waste additional funds.

Plaintiffs have also argued that, if the additional resources available in wealthy school districts are of such little value, a system that allocates substantially more resources to some districts is inherently wasteful and irrational and that, if defendants really believe their arguments, they would not cling to a financial system that affords a substantial resource advantage to wealthy districts.

In the next section, we will consider how the courts have dealt with educational productivity research and the arguments of the parties in resolving constitutional challenges to school finance systems.

How the Courts Have Responded to Educational Productivity Issues

The written decisions of courts that have decided constitutional challenges to state school finance systems reflect a reluctance to rely on educational productivity research. In general, this holds true whether the courts have ruled for plaintiffs and struck down these systems, or whether they have ruled for defendants and upheld the systems. Rather, judicial analysis has focused on expenditure inequalities among school districts, the resultant inequalities in educational resources, the causes of these inequalities, and the justification asserted by states for these inequalities, that is, whether they serve some legitimate state interest.

A close reading of the cases indicates that courts generally have assumed that significant inequalities in educational resources have consequences for the education of children in ways that often cannot be measured accurately. As a result, the courts have placed the burden on defendants to show that these inequalities are demonstrably irrelevant to children.

An ultimate factual question for most courts has been whether school finance systems discriminate in the allocation of educational opportunities among school districts. In most cases, the major inquiry has been into differences in educational inputs available to students in districts that have differing financial resources.

Connecticut: **Horton *v.* Meskill.** In *Horton* v. *Meskill* the Connecticut Supreme Court found that unequal educational opportunities resulting from heavy reliance on the unequal property wealth of school districts were discriminatory and unconstitutional under the Connecticut state constitution. Most of the court's criteria for comparing educational opportunity relate to educational inputs: "(a) size of classes; (b) training, experience, and background of teaching staff; (c) materials, books, and supplies; (d) school philosophy and objectives; (e) type of local control; (f) test scores as measured against ability; (g) degree of motivation and application of the students; (h) course offerings and extracurricular activities" (*Horton,* 1977, at 368).

Local control was considered an input, because the evidence showed that the greater financial resources of wealthy districts necessarily gave them more choices in implementing educational objectives. Although test scores and degree of motivation and application of students were also included as aspects of educational opportunity, and although defendants produced witnesses on the ambiguity of educational productivity research, these did not figure significantly in the decision, which found "a direct relationship between per-pupil school expenditures and the breadth and quality of educational programs" (*Horton,* 1977, at 368).

New Jersey: **Robinson v. Cahill.** The New Jersey Supreme Court saw a direct connection between educational resources and opportunities in *Robinson* v. *Cahill.* This early decision held the New Jersey school finance system unconstitutional for failing to provide a thorough and efficient system of education as required by the state constitution. The court found that the constitutional mandate required "equal educational opportunities."

The court noted that there had been testimony on the "correlation between dollar input per pupil and the end product of the educational process" and that "equality of dollar input will not assure equality in educational results"; however, the court found that "it is nonetheless clear that there is a significant connection between the sums expended and the quality of educational opportunity" (*Robinson,* 1976, at 277). For the court, the relevant inquiry was what the government provides, not how well each child profits from these resources.

The Connecticut and New Jersey cases do not discuss who has the burden of dealing with the relationship between educational inputs and outputs, but it is clear that the courts in both cases assumed that inputs were the correct measure of educational opportunities, absent a conclusive showing to the contrary. The most explicit indication that plaintiffs need not prove this relationship is found in the decisions of the California courts in *Serrano* v. *Priest.*

California: **Serrano v. Priest.** The first *Serrano* decision (1971) came before a trial had been held. The California court did not at this time find the California school finance system unconstitutional. Rather, it returned the case to the lower court for trial. One of the issues for trial was whether different levels of educational expenditures affect the quality of education (*Serrano,* 1971, at 487; 1976, at 1253, no. 16). At trial, the defendants made the input-output issue a major part of their case, and both sides produced evidence on the issue.

However, after summarizing the extensive record on educational productivity, the trial court concluded that "the appropriate standard for measuring the quality of education being provided the pupils of a school district is the school-district-offerings standard rather than the pupil-achievement standard" (*Serrano,* 1974, at 99–100). Using this standard, the court found significant differences in the quality of educational opportunities available in high-wealth and low-wealth school districts.

The shift of the burden to defendants on the educational productivity issue is also apparent in this decision. The court noted that the evidence clearly showed that high-spending districts could not be reduced to the per-pupil expenditure of poor districts without affecting the quality of their educational programs adversely, and the court concluded: "That per-pupil expenditures play no part in pupil achievement on standardized tests is simply not supported by any credible evidence" (*Serrano,* 1974, at 90). Thus, to the extent that educational productivity research was relevant at all, the burden was for defendants to disprove that resources and educational quality were linked, rather than for plaintiffs to prove it. That is, based on the conflicting evidence on educational productivity research, the trial court found that educational resources have an effect on students' scores on standardized tests, but the court made it clear that this finding was of little significance for resolving the constitutional issues on the case (*Serrano,* 1974, at 94). These trial court findings were affirmed by the California court in *Serrano* (1976).

Wyoming: **Washakie v. Herschler.** This shift of the burden to disprove a relationship between educational resources and quality is also found in a recent decision of the Wyoming Supreme Court, which held that state's school finance system unconstitutional (*Washakie* v. *Herschler,* 1980, at 32). The court's words there are worth quoting: "It would be unacceptable logic to deduce that the wealthy counties are squandering their money merely from the fact that poorer counties are getting along just fine and providing an adequate education on the lesser amounts per child they have. For the state and the wealthy districts to put forth the assertion that money is not everything is making just such an argument. . . . It is nothing more than an illusion to believe that the extensive disparity in financial resources does not relate directly to quality of education."

It is of great significance that courts that have ruled against plaintiffs and found funding systems to be constitutional have also applied an input or educational offering standard to judge the effects of school finance systems. These courts have accepted that children are harmed by receiving fewer educational resources. Their point of departure from plaintiffs' claims has been not on the conclusion of harm suffered by the children but on the willingness of the courts to do anything about it.

Georgia: **Thomas** *v.* **Stewart.** The foregoing point is illustrated by the recent decision of the Georgia Supreme Court in *Thomas* v. *Stewart,* which overturned the trial court's finding of unconstitutionality. While upholding the finance system on legal grounds, the court stated that in Georgia "there is a direct relationship between a district's level of funding and the educational opportunities which a school district is able to provide its children." (*Thomas,* 1981, at 8). Further, it considered "unassailable" the trial court's conclusion that the inequalities in educational opportunities resulting from disparities among school districts in taxable property wealth "deny students in property-poor school districts equal educational opportunities" (*Thomas,* 1981, at 9). The Georgia Supreme Court agreed with defendants' ultimate conclusion that the system was not unconstitutional, but it did not agree with defendants' arguments that unequal resources made little difference to the education of children. What the court found was that unequal educational opportunities do not violate the Georgia constitution.

Oregon: Olsen **v.** *State.* An earlier decision by the Oregon Supreme Court came to a similar conclusion (*Olsen,* 1976, at 146). Based on evidence comparing educational inputs in many school districts, the court noted that poor districts had "substantial deficiencies in educational opportunities." This was not of significance to the court, since it found that the Oregon constitution only required a minimum basic education.

Texas: Supreme Court Decision in **Rodriguez.** There are, however, two exceptions to the general rule that educational productivity issues have not been significant in the resolution of school finance cases. The first is the United States Supreme Court's decision in *San Antonio Independent School District* v. *Rodriguez.* The second is *Thompson* v. *Engelking,* which was decided by the Idaho Supreme Court. Of particular interest is that no evidence was produced at trial in either case on the educational productivity research; both courts went outside the official record for information on this issue.

In *San Antonio Independent School District* v. *Rodriguez,* the Supreme Court noted the controversy over the extent to which there is a demonstrable correlation "between educational expenditures and the quality of education" to bolster its conclusion to uphold the Texas school finance system, citing articles on both sides of the argument (*San Antonio Independent School District,* 1973, at 43). The significance of this point is unclear, since it appears to be used by the court simply to corroborate its conclusion not to examine expenditure inequalities produced by the Texas system of school finance closely. In addition, the evidence in the case focused on expenditure inequalities, not on the resulting inequalities in particular educational inputs. Consequently, it is unclear whether the court's concern with the unresolved controversy refers to the lack of necessary information on the impact of expenditure differences on both inputs and outputs or solely to the educational productivity issue. In any case, the educational productivity issue was not the pivotal point here.

Idaho: **Thompson** *v.* **Engelking.** In *Thompson* v. *Engelking,* the trial court had found "a significant connection between sums spent on education and the quality of educational opportunity." In reversing the trial court's holding that the Idaho finance system was unconstitutional, the Idaho Supreme Court rejected this factual finding. The Supreme Court did so on the basis of an unnamed reference dealing with educational productivity issues, from which it concluded that "because of this ongoing argument as to the relationship of funds expended per pupil... to the quality of educational opportunity," it would refuse to look closely at the expenditure inequalities resulting from the state's school finance system (*Thompson,* 1975, at 642). However, the material on which the court relied (the Coleman Report), was not in evidence, and plaintiffs were given no opportunity to respond. As a result, two dissenting justices (this was a three-to-two decision) accused the majority of injudicious conduct for going outside the record and for misrepresenting the educational productivity research as concluding that expenditures have no effect on a child's education (*Thompson,* 1975, at 666).

Current Legal Trends

It is particularly significant that neither the *Rodriguez* nor the *Engelking* court, both of which relied on educational productivity research to rule against plaintiffs, had the benefit of witnesses or exhibits describing the research or of cross-examination to elicit its limitations. In contrast, all the courts in which defendants and plaintiffs presented extended evidence on educational productivity issues through expert witnesses and exhibits found the issue to be of little importance in resolving the ultimate issue of the constitutionality of the state's school finance system. Indeed, several of the courts in which educational productivity issues were heavily contested found that educational resources can have a positive impact on educational outputs, including achievement. We are not sure what significance can be ascribed either to these correlations or to the additional fact that, in every case in which the educational productivity issue was extensively considered at trial, the court found the school finance system constitutionally deficient; however, they do create a notable pattern and constitute the clear trend of the law.

Some courts, including the California courts in *Serrano,* have concluded, after hearing witnesses on both sides, that there are positive relationships between input measures and scores on achievement tests. For example, a New York appellate court recently affirmed trial court findings that adequately funded and staffed remedial programs can alleviate or remedy the learning problems of many children who fail in school (*Levittown,* 1981, at 36). In a Colorado school finance case, the trial court concluded after extensive testimony that it is "more probable, rather than less probable" that achievement test scores are related to a variety of input measures (*Luhan,* 1979, at 36). However, as in *Serrano,* this finding was not essential to the result, which was based primarily on inequalities in educational resources among school districts.

In *Rodriguez,* the Supreme Court expressed concern that a holding that the Texas school finance system was unconstitutional "could circumscribe or handicap the continued research and experimentation so vital to finding even partial solutions to educational problems and to keeping abreast of ever-changing conditions" (*San Antonio Independent School District,* 1973, at 43). Implicit in this comment is a belief that plaintiffs in these cases are seeking to impose restraints on the allocation of resources that are educationally unsound or that would prevent the application of insights about deployment of resources to maximize the likelihood of achievement gains for particular children. Here, the Supreme Court evidences a fundamental misconception of plaintiffs' claims.

Typically, plaintiffs have sought only to bar factors that have nothing to do with education, such as the size of the local tax base, from determining the level of resources in a given school district. While plaintiffs would end inequalities in educational resources that result from unequal local wealth, in no case have plaintiffs sought a simple equal dollar or equal inputs solution. Indeed, the major objective of these cases has been to require the use of factors legitimately related to education in the allocation of educational funds, with the knowledge that this could mean unequal allocation of dollars. For example, a state could provide more funds for handicapped children, remedial programs, vocational education, or early childhood education and take into account the differing costs of providing the same inputs in different school districts. It could also allocate and require the use of funds in a manner advised by educational productivity research. In summary, ending discrimination in the allocation of resources that results from noneducational factors does not preclude making distinctions among school districts and children based upon educational criteria.

Since *Rodriguez,* courts that have held school finance systems unconstitutional have recognized the limited scope of plaintiffs' challenges. In *Horton* v. *Meskill,* for example, the Connecticut Supreme Court noted that "the very uncertainty of the extent of the nexus between dollar input and quality of educational opportunity requires allowance for variances as to individual and group disadvantages and local conditions" (*Horton,* 1977, at 376). The New Jersey Supreme Court, in *Robinson,* ruling shortly after *Rodriguez,* adverted to area cost differences and additional inputs for disadvantaged children (*Robinson,* 1976, at 298). In *Washakie,* the Wyoming Supreme Court indicated approval of allocation formulas that "compensate for special needs — educational cost differentials. . . . We [the court] only proscribe any system which makes the quality of a child's education a function of district wealth. We hold that exact or absolute equality is not required. There must be allowance for variances in individuals, groups and local conditions." Then, the court stated: "All precedents are in accord on this proposition" (*Washakie,* 1980, at 34).

With very few exceptions, the courts that have reviewed school finance systems have not considered educational productivity issues to be of major importance for resolving constitutional issues. The central issue has been the rationality of a system that allocates educational resources on the basis of factors that have nothing to do with education. The fact that researchers debate the effect of educational resources on standardized achievement test scores has not dissuaded courts from concluding that the discriminatory allocation of resources is fundamentally unfair. This was clearly articulated by a Maryland court that recently held the Maryland school finance system unconstitutional: "Uncertainty about the degree to which the amount of money makes a difference in the quality of education. . . [does not] under any conceivable set of circumstances justify unequal distribution of those funds" (*Somerset,* 1981, at 34). Courts, no less than parents, are unwilling to place children at risk, pending the eventual outcome of this research. In addition, court decisions that have held school financing systems unconstitutional do not prohibit states from applying the insights of educational productivity research in the deployment of educational resources, since the primary concern of these cases has been to require states to use factors relating to education in the allocation of educational resources.

Possible Future Directions

One possible direction to which recent educational productivity research appears to point lies in the use of a medical model of treatment. As already noted, such research has begun to show that identical resources do not have the same effect on every child. A medical model would prescribe additional educational resources, different educational resources, or both, based on the general likelihood that these resources would produce positive results — and on the recognition that individual children with similar measurable characteristics will respond differently to the same treatment. Consequently, the progress of individual children would have to be monitored and evaluated so that different treatments could be tried for children who did not respond to the first treatment. This medical diagnosis and treatment model is currently required for handicapped children under the Education of All Handicapped Children Act, P.L. 94–142.

Plaintiffs in school finance cases have not sought to require that this model be applied to all children. However, this line of educational productivity research, which shows that resources have differential effects on children, supports plaintiffs' contention that educational resources can make a difference, and it may have a contribution to make as constitutional educational finance systems are designed.

References

Coleman, J. S., and others. *Equality of Educational Opportunity.* Washington, D. C.: National Center for Education Statistics, Office of Education, 1966.

Horton versus *Meskill,* 172 Conn. 615, 376 A.2d 359 (1977).

Levittown versus *Nquist,* Slip Opinion (Supreme Court, Appellate Division, Second Judicial Department, October 26, 1981).

Luhan versus *Colorado,* Slip Opinion (D.Ct. Denver, March 31, 1979).

Murnane, R. J. *The Impact of School Resources on the Learning of Inner City Children.* Cambridge, Mass.: Ballinger, 1975.

Olsen versus *State,* 276 Or. 9, 554 P.2d 139 (1976).

San Antonio Independent School District versus *Rodriguez,* 411 U.S. 1 (1973).

Serrano versus *Priest,* 5 Cal. 3d 584, 487 1241 (1971).

Serrano versus *Priest,* Slip Opinion (Superior Court of Los Angeles County, April 10, 1974).

Serrano versus *Priest,* 18 Cal. 3d 728, 557 P.2d 929 (1976).

Somerset versus *Hornbeck,* Slip Opinion (Circuit Court of Baltimore, May 19, 1981).

Summers, A. A., and Wolfe, B. L. "Do Schools Make a Difference?" *American Economic Review,* 1977, *67* (4), 639–652.

Thomas versus *Stewart,* 285 S.E.2d 156 (Georgia Supreme Court, 1981).

Thompson versus *Engelking,* 96 Ida. 795, 537 P.2d 635 (1975).

Washakie versus *Herschler,* Wyo., 606 P.2d 310, cert. denied 101 S.Ct. 86 (1980).

David C. Long and Sandra H. McMullan are attorneys with the law firm of Long and Silverstein, P.C., Washington, D.C. The firm specializes in matters relating to education, children, and handicapped persons. David Long has represented plaintiffs in school finance cases in Colorado, Georgia, Arkansas, New Jersey, and West Virginia. Sandra McMullan was one of the plaintiffs' attorneys in the Maryland school finance case, Somerset *versus* Hornbeck.

In the Philadelphia school district, in 1975–1976, several
educational inputs, including the basal linguistic approach,
were particularly distinguishable for their contribution to growth
in the reading achievement of fourth graders.

What Helps Fourth
Grade Students to Read?

Anita A. Summers
Mark J. Raivetz

This chapter describes an education production function study conducted in
the School District of Philadelphia. Another study (Summers and Wolfe,
1974, 1975, 1977) was its catalyst. The major objective of this study was to
identify school inputs, particularly those over which the school administration
had control, that affected fourth-grade reading achievement.

The search for evidence on what works was aided by an extraordinarily
rich data base, which included pupil-specific data (the number of absences
and race, for example), classroom-specific data (how reading groups were organized, the number of minutes spent in independent reading, and teacher
characteristics, for example), and program-specific data (the reading approach
that was used, the number of teaching aides involved, and whether the program was being used for the first time). The richness of the data made it pos-

Michael H. Kean, executive director of research and evaluation in the School
District of Philadelphia until 1981, coordinated the project; Irvin J. Farber, director of
evaluation services, was an active and essential participant in its planning and implementation.

A. Summers (Ed.). *New Directions for Testing and Measurement: Productivity Assessment in Education,* no. 15.
San Francisco: Jossey-Bass, September 1982.

sible to examine interactions between inputs and pupil characteristics, to explore nonlinear specifications, to use a change specification for the dependent variable, and to separate the original sample into two parts — one used in developing the specification, the other in testing it.

The results of this exploration suggest that one reading approach — the linguistic basal approach — is clearly most effective in the sample, that direct contact time between teacher and pupil is productive, that the student body composition is associated with learning, and that there is no evidence of productivity for many characteristics of the professional staff that are rewarded. Further, the results suggest that, when regression coefficients are to be used as guides for policy, replication procedures should be employed. Fewer recommendations may emerge, but they can be stated with greater conviction.

It should be noted that a joint effort by an urban school district that was largely preoccupied with daily crises and an economist who was largely preoccupied with public finance and econometric interests required a great deal of cooperation. It was the coincidence of interest in the results that made the process work.

The following sections describe sample selection, choice of variables and collection of data, model and estimation procedures, results, and policy implications.

Sample Selection

The School District of Philadelphia felt strongly that schools in the sample had to reflect a visibly wide range of average test scores. The fact that regression analysis does not require the sample distribution of the dependent variable to match the corresponding population distribution did not, in their view, counter the political requirements of visible representation of all types of schools.

The following procedure was used, therefore, to determine the schools from which the study sample was drawn: First, the 1974 average Total Reading Achievement Development Scale Score (ADSS) on the California Achievement Test (CAT-70) were summed over grades one to four for all 190 elementary schools in the district. The same process was repeated with the 1975 average Total Reading ADSS CAT-70 scores. Then, schools were ordered on the basis of the difference of these sums, and the schools that ranked 1–15, 89–103, and 176–190 were identified. The schools were similarly ordered on the basis of their February 1975 Total Reading ADSS CAT for grades one through four and ranked 1–15, 89–103, and 176–190. The two schools that appeared in both high-achievement and high-gain groups and the two schools that appeared in both low-achievement and low-gain groups were selected for the sample. Then, schools were selected as high if they were in the top quarter in achievement and the top third in gain; as middle if they were in both the achievement and gain middle groups; and as low if they were in the bottom quarter in achievement and the bottom third in gain. Finally, schools, when closely ranked, were selected to provide representation from all eight administrative subdistricts in the city.

The final sample contained ten high, five middle, and ten low schools. These schools were regarded as representative of schools having students who exhibited high, middle, and low degrees of success in reading achievement and of a geographical cross section of the city. All fourth graders in these twenty-five schools became subjects in the study.

Grade four students were selected as an important target group for several reasons. First, the School District of Philadelphia regards this grade as an important point at which to identify trouble. Second, it is the highest grade that permits all elementary school pupils to be potential subjects. Since Philadelphia elementary schools are organized in a number of grade configurations (K–4, K–5, K–6, K–7, K–8), selection of a higher grade would have eliminated some school organizations and thereby reduced the ability to examine the impact of school organization on learning. Third, the grade three score was selected as the pretest score because the Level One CAT-70 test used in grades one and two had problems in the norms tables; that is, the fiftieth percentile in grade one comprehension is one item above guessing level. Students in both grades three and four are given the Level Two test, so that both their achievement levels and their growth scores could be used. Fourth, public attention has been focused on this grade, because the test scores have declined over the years. Fifth, methodological concerns about not examining multiple outputs can be reduced by studying an early grade, where cognitive skills receive primary emphasis.

The final sample, then, consisted of 1,828 students who were in the fourth grade in 1975–76. These students were distributed among twenty-five elementary schools, and they had twenty-five principals, twenty-five reading teachers, ninety-four classroom teachers, and sixty-eight reading aides.

Choice of Variables and Collection of Data

The question of concern involved fourth-grade reading, so the choice set of dependent variables was narrow. Ideally, theories would be available to help in selection of the independent variables. No solid body of accepted theories exists in this area, however, so the choice was wide.

Choice of Variables. The dependent variable selected was the scaled score change on the Reading Comprehension subtest of the California Achievement Test (CAT-70) for each pupil between February 1975 (third grade) and February 1976 (fourth grade). School district personnel were unwilling to use the Total Reading score from the CAT, because they had found inadequate sensitivity in the norm tables for the score in another subtest, Vocabulary, with students who were above the fiftieth percentile. The use of test scores as an output measure has regularly been the subject of concern. The fact remains, however, that the public increasingly views test scores as measures of how schools and school districts are doing, and test scores are being used as a major criterion in determining the path of future schooling.

The change formulation was used for three reasons: First, policy recommendations do not start from a zero base, so a formulation that reflected marginal impacts seemed more appropriate that one that did not. Second, the use of a value-added measure conforms to the usual choice in estimating production functions in economics. Third, although there was a significantly negative correlation between initial score and change in achievement, the omission of initial score from the regression did not change the significance or magnitude of the coefficients in any important way.

One hundred and sixty-two independent variables were measured. They were organized into five groups: characteristics of students, including race, sex, and block income (a special procedure for estimating block income is described by Summers and Wolfe, 1978); characteristics of principals, including experience as a principal, race, sex, and experience as a reading teacher; school characteristics, including capacity, enrollment, racial composition, and grade organization; teacher characteristics, including educational background, experience, teaching strategies, and attendance; and characteristics of reading instruction, including reading approach, student grouping, and teacher preference for the approach.

The main interest of the study for the School District of Philadelphia was the insight that could be obtained about the four reading approaches used in the program. Twelve different commercial programs were used in the ninety-four classrooms studied. These twelve programs can be grouped into four approaches. The specific skills approach involves giving differents sets of recommended materials to students at varied levels in response to perceived need; materials cover the areas of decoding, study skills, comprehension, and literature, while various published and teacher-made programs are used to supplement basic reading instruction in the classroom. The traditional basal approach uses a graded series of readers as its basic component, together with supplementary materials; basals begin with the development of sight vocabulary and generally feature controlled vocabulary and skills, with emphasis on comprehension. The linguistic basal approach, which uses a graded series of readers as its basic component, emphasizes phonics first, then comprehension; words are presented in groups based on sound-symbol relationships, with short vowels usually introduced first. Finally, the linguistic programmed approach is basically a linguistic approach with a strong emphasis on decoding; materials are presented in small steps (frames), a response is required from the learner, and immediate feedback is provided; comprehension materials are used, but very little at first.

Educational production functions have been criticized by educators and sociologists for their failure to include organizational and process measurements. Whenever quantification occurs, much is left out. There is an underlying assumption that, if the right-hand variables are reproduced, the left-hand variables will be reproduced. The study described here attempted to incorporate more process and organizational variables. But, it still is true that filling a paint-by-number canvas does not result in a Rembrandt.

Collection of Data. Once the list of independent variables had been determined, five data collection instruments were designed. One was merely a keypunching form to permit efficient recording of data from individual pupil records. The other four were interview protocols: a principal interview, involving questions on the principal's professional development and management of the school reading program; a reading teacher interview, involving questions of the teacher's professional development, the school district's climate of support, and the reading teacher's services to the school; a classroom reading aide interview, involving questions on the aide's background and the services provided; and a classroom teacher interview, involving questions on the teacher's professional development, the school district's climate of support, the classroom's organization and practices, and the reading materials used. The first drafts of these instruments were pilot-tested in several schools that were not in the sample of twenty-five and revisions were made.

The School District of Philadelphia had a number of concerns. Whenever possible, unobtrusive approaches were preferred, with minimization of personal contact a major objective. The fact that the school year was drawing to a close when the data were being collected dictated the use of many data collectors. Fifteen minutes was regarded as the maximum time for administration of a questionnaire. (A school district maxim was that the amount of cooperation that could be expected from schools was inversely related to the amount of disruption caused!) Questions had to be framed so that individuals would be not only able but willing to answer. Questions could not be worded so that the only possible answers were the socially acceptable ones. Beyond this, questions were addressed, as much as possible, to the recipients of services.

Data collection teams assigned to the twenty-five schools in the study were composed of staff from the district's Office of Research and Evaluation and reading program staff from central and district offices. Depending on the size of the school, teams spent between one-half day and two days interviewing school personnel and recording data from pupil records. In all cases, principals and classroom teachers were interviewed by Office of Research and Evaluation personnel. The task of interviewing reading aides and reading teachers was shared with personnel from the Division of Reading. In some cases, team members covered classes, so that teachers could be interviewed. Information concerning pupils was copied from school records on the forms developed for the project.

Administrators and teachers were generally very cooperative, which enabled the entire data collection process to be completed in less than two weeks. Next questionnaires were examined for completeness, reduced and coded where necessary, and examined again. Not only were questionnaires of the same type compared with one another, but all four types of questionnaires in each school were examined for consistency. Control questions were inserted into the questionnaires for consistency checking.

Once the data were complete for all 1,828 fourth-grade students, the sample was broken into two parts, an experimental file and a cross-validation file. So large and rich a data base made cross-validation possible. Before a single regression equation was formulated, the final random sample file was run with a program that selected every fourth case. The resulting 465 students were placed on a separate tape. There they "rested," untouched by man or machine, while an experimental file of 1,363 students was mined extensively. Only after the final "best fit" equation had been run and recorded was the cross-validation file accessed. The results of both the experimental sample and the cross-validation sample form the basis for the findings on fourth-grade reading achievement in the School District of Philadelphia.

Model and Estimation Procedures

In conducting research, the standard scientific procedure is to state a theory, obtain the appropriate data for each theoretical concept involved, and test the theory empirically, using standard tests of significance as guideposts for measuring success. It is no accident, however, that most writers of doctoral dissertations in economics and education first obtain some data which they proceed to examine before they write the chapter on theory. The fact is that in many areas of education, as in many areas of economics, there is no solid body of theory upon which to draw, and the data are far from ideal in reflecting theoretical concepts. The standard scientific procedure, therefore, needs to be revised to accommodate the realities of the discipline. Theil (1971), and Christ (1966) both made recommendations of this sort.

In the Philadelphia study, which examined the determinants of growth in reading achievement, there was no one agreed upon body of theory to test.

As a result, we were forced to use an alternative way both of arriving at a theoretical model and of testing it. These were the steps that were taken: First, we looked at data from a sample of 1,363 students; that is, these data were mined extensively in an experimental sample. The resulting equation was regarded as the theory—the hypothesized relationship between growth in students' reading achievement between the third and fourth grades and many inputs. Next, t tests were run on the coefficients; however, these were used only as general guideposts, since the data had already been mined. Then, the theory—the regression equation resulting from the mining—was tested on a randomly selected, totally unexplored sample of 465 students from the same population of students—the cross-validation sample. Finally, tests were run to examine the equality of the coefficients between the two samples. The final conclusions and policy implications were drawn from the two sets of regression results, from the tests on the equality of the coefficients, and from a liberal interpretation of the coefficients and the standard tests of significance.

The model that was developed was of the general form $\Delta R = F$ (KID, PRIN, SCHL, TEACH, READ). That is, the combined wisdom of the literature on reading achievement and of School District of Philadelphia personnel who were responsible for designing and monitoring the reading programs suggested that reading growth between the third and fourth grades (ΔR) is a critical educational junction and that it is a function of many characteristics of the pupil (KID), characteristics of the school principal (PRIN), characteristics that described the atmosphere of the school (SCHL), characteristics of the student's teacher (TEACH), and characteristics of the reading program and the way in which it was delivered to the students (READ).

The relationship was examined using single-equation multiple regressions. In the experimental sample, dummy variables and other nonlinearities were explored. Interactions of pupil achievement with other inputs were examined extensively, consistent with the regularly stated theory that students of different abilities react differently to the characteristics of their schools, their peers, their teachers, and their skills program. All the findings were checked and rechecked against alternative specifications for robustness, and only the variables that remained strong throughout the mining process were retained. (Tables listing all the variables examined, the sources of the data, the means and standard deviations of the variables, and details of the regression results are available from the authors.)

Results

A pragmatic regression strategy calls for use of all the empirical results in the final interpretation. Many results emerged from the extensive empirical analysis. They should be useful to educational policy makers in the School District of Philadelphia, and they may be suggestive to staff of other school districts. (Tables describing the data and regression results are available from the authors.)

Impact of Pupil Characteristics. Which characteristics of students over which the school district has some control can contribute to fourth-grade reading growth? Regular attendance clearly increases the probability that a student will have an increase in reading scores between the third and fourth grades greater than students who attend fewer days. (A good case can be made for treating school attendance and unexcused absences as dependent variables. Reverse causality seems somewhat tenuous, however, since elementary school children are usually unaware of their standardized test scores. And, when the equations were estimated without these variables, the remaining coefficients were not changed in a way that altered the conclusions.)

With somewhat less conviction—because of the lesser robustness of the coefficients throughout the exploration of the experimental sample—one can say that attending kindergarten and having fewer unexcused absences contribute to fourth-grade reading growth. It is clear that the higher a student's third-grade reading score, the less that student's fourth-grade reading growth will be. Apart from the stardard explanation of regression toward the mean, there is a general view that students who whiz through the first three years slump in the fourth grade.

Equally important to note are pupil characteristics that were found to be without significance: pupil's family income, pupil busing to relieve overcrowding, pupil's number of residences while in school, and kindergarten attendance at the same or a different school.

Impact of Principal Characteristics. One of the more interesting results of the Philadelphia study is the evidence that it provides on the impact of a principal's involvement in reading on reading achievement. Fourth-grade students of principals who were reading professionals achieved more reading growth than students of principals who were not. It has been suggested that the explanation lies in the fact that such a principal is likely to be an active instructional leader in the area. Because he or she is conversant with the subject, reading and classroom teachers and the principal speak the same language, and students benefit from such exchange. In addition, the evidence of the Philadelphia study is that the more time that a principal spends observing fourth-grade reading classes, the greater the students' development. The message is clear: Involvement by elementary principals in reading instruction has a payoff in reading achievement growth.

Many other characteristics of principals were examined and found to be without significance: previous administrative experience, amount of consultation received from reading program publishers and district office staff, elementary school teaching certification, principal's highest degree, number of years as a classroom teacher, number of years in the school, number of years as a principal, and perceptions about home support and teacher expertise.

Impact of School Characteristics. The combined evidence of the results indicates strongly that students in schools with more supportive staff per pupil and with fewer nonwhite students are more likely to achieve greater fourth-grade reading growth. Clearly, here as elsewhere, direct cause-and-effect conclusions are inappropriate. We do not know whether the fact that there are more supportive personnel per pupil is of direct help to students or whether the characteristics of the school that resulted in a higher ratio is the helping agent. Similarly, the relationship between the racial mix of the school and fourth-grade reading growth may well be explained by a set of affective characteristics associated with that mix which is not picked up by the other variables.

A slightly less strong finding, but a very robust one throughout the exploration of the experimental sample, is the negative impact of a K–6 organization, compared with the alternatives. A K–5 organization, compared with a K–8 organization makes no difference, but K–7 seems to be superior to K–8. The evidence of this study suggests that, in terms of impact on reading growth, K–7 is best, K–5 and K–8 are about the same, and K–6 is distinctly inferior.

The results also indicate fairly strongly that students in schools with more high achievers do better, although the very high-achieving students are not affected by this aspect of the school climate. Less strong, but not to be ignored, is the finding that fourth-grade reading growth is negatively associated with being in a school with more very new teachers and that it is the students at grade level and above who are most affected; however, it seems to be irrelevant to students distinctly below grade level.

School characteristics that were found not to be significant include: median income of the school feeder areas, proportion of students from families on AFDC, proportion of students below the sixteenth percentile, proportion of nonwhite professional staff, and mobility of the school population.

Impact of Teacher Characteristics. The qualities of a teacher that contribute to success for fourth-grade readers must be many, but only a few of them are readily quantifiable. Of these quantifiable characteristics our findings indicate strongly that the presence of a teacher (as opposed to some sort of substitute) is important: Students who had teachers with more pay periods with no absences did distinctly better, as did students who had teachers who attended fewer outside conferences. And, students whose teacher was teaching the fourth grade for the first time did distinctly worse.

The evidence that female teachers are associated with increased fourth-grade reading achievement is less strong. There is a slight suggestion that male students do better with female teachers and that female students do better with male teachers.

A large number of other teacher characteristics were found not to be significant: the Gourman (1967) rating of teacher's undergraduate school, number of graduate reading and language arts courses taken, National Teachers' Examination score, race, number of years as a classroom teacher, whether the teacher was teaching in the present school for the first time, whether the teacher had requested assignment to the present school, and whether teachers had been involved in development of the school reading plan.

Impact of Reading Instruction Characteristics. The evidence that a number of characteristics of reading instruction are strongly associated with fourth-grade reading growth seems compelling. The more minutes per week spent on individual independent reading, the better. If the classroom teacher uses fewer aides per week, there is more growth in reading scores. Finally, students of teachers who say they would select the particular reading program again are likely to show more reading improvement than students of teachers who do not—a reflection of teacher confidence, perhaps.

Most interesting of all, the linguistic basal approach produces better fourth-grade reading growth for students at or above grade level than the three other approaches used in the School District of Philadelphia—specific skills, traditional basal, or programmed linguistic. Probably no finding in the study was more robust than this. Many alternative specifications were examined, but the linguistic basal approach was always associated with higher rates of learning. Low-achieving students were not helped more by one type of program than by another.

The class size debate must continue. In the Philadelphia study, the evidence is that students do better in larger classes. Alternatives specifications— nonlinear and interactive—were extensively explored, but the finding remains. Certainly, many studies point to the opposite finding, but others point to this one. In interpreting the finding, however, it is important to emphasize that it emerges when many other variables are controlled—that is, the positive coefficients are saying that larger classes are better, after such instructional characteristics as the degree of individualization is controlled for.

There is extensive discussion in the literature on the right grouping for reading instruction. The findings for fourth graders in the School District of Philadelphia is that students who are taught reading in a class where only individualized or only small-group instruction is used do not do as well as students who are taught where there is some large grouping in the room. Students in classes where a mixture of individual and small-group instruction is used to teach reading do as well as students in classes with some large groupings, and they do better than students in classes where there is only individual or only small-group instruction. One interpretation of these results is that, again, the teacher's active presence plays a decisive role. One possible reason why individual and small-group instruction are both less effective is that the teacher can then only be involved with a few students at a time, while the teacher is actively involved with more students more of the time in large-group instruction.

Finally, there was a strong suggestion in the experimental sample that certain positive things happen when a program is used for the first time. Reading specialists have suggested that teachers pay much stricter attention to the instructions associated with a reading program during the first year. However, the cross-validation sample did not support this hypothesis.

Many other characteristics of reading instruction were found not to be significant, including: number of minutes per day of reading instruction, time of day when reading was taught, number of years that the reading teacher had been a classroom teacher, number of reading and language arts courses taken by the reading teacher, professional development methods (outside visits to reading programs, attendance at seminars, participation in professional organizations), consultation from district office staff and reading program publisher, and specific ways in which the reading teacher helps the classroom teacher (to structure the classroom, to demonstrate techniques, to provide professional information).

The conclusion that emerges is that the choice of reading approach makes a difference to all but the very low achievers and that the active, direct efforts and time of the teacher (not substitutes for the teacher) make a significant difference.

Summary. The findings of most immediate interest to policy makers are those over which they have some control. What does this study say about issues with which educators are concerned?

The study explored a single issue: growth in fourth-grade reading achievement as measured by changes in standardized test scores. Many studies in the literature document the problems to be encountered in any precise reading of the statistical results of this type of education production function investigation. For that reason, the intent here is to interpret the findings in a broad, directional manner — that is, to indicate the positive or negative effect on only the robust findings, not to suggest that we know the precise degree to which reading scores can be altered by altering a given input by a specified amount. While the caveats are being laid out, it is also important to keep in mind that the study has been done only with students in the School District of Philadelphia. This study has shown better than previous studies, what is effective with them, because of the extensive classroom-, program-, and pupil-specific data that we had and because of the regression strategy that we used in analyzing the data. It remains for others to test our hypotheses in other school districts.

Policy Implications

The study has yielded considerable information about reading that top management and key decision makers of the School District of Philadelphia might find to be both interesting and useful. There are several major implications for policy:

First, spending more days in school is associated with learning — probably because it is a signal of pupil motivation and because things happen in school that make being there important to learning. For either reason, attendance records are important measures of the success of programs and how they are implemented.

Second, neither frequency of residential moves nor busing undertaken to relieve overcrowding is associated with poorer learning. These factors may have other detrimental effects, but the evidence does not point to effects on fourth-grade reading.

Third, involvement of elementary school principals in reading, through previous professional training in reading and current observation, is associated with greater learning. If fourth-grade reading growth is important, then there is a case for paying attention to these characteristics of principals — rather than to such characteristics as degrees, experience, consultation, sex, or race, none of which is visibly associated with learning.

Fourth, organization of elementary schools in a K-7 format seems most effective for fourth-grade reading development, compared with the alternatives. The K-6 format is associated with less learning. Schools with more supportive staff per pupil also are more effective. Frequently, additional supportive staff are funded with money from federal sources, which suggests that such money is well spent.

Fifth, student body composition is associated with learning, in the sense that low- and middle-achieving students do better in schools with fewer nonwhite pupils. Translating this finding into policy, however, seems inappropriate. The contribution that changes in student body composition could make to fourth-grade reading achievement is clearly only a small portion of the major policy objectives.

Sixth, the median income of the school feeder area, the proportion of students from families on AFDC, and the proportion of students below the sixteenth percentile do not help to predict fourth-grade learning. The policy implication of this finding is important. It suggests that allocation of federal funds on the basis of schoolwide low-income and low-achievement characteristics is not appropriate, if the object is to help disadvantaged students. Targeting has to be pupil-specific.

Seventh, increased fourth-grade reading growth is associated with increased direct contact between student and teacher, which in turn is associated with fewer personal or professional absences taken from teaching time. This suggests that educational procedures and rewards that increase such contact are likely to benefit learning. Very new teachers, it would appear, operate to the disadvantage of fourth-grade readers; this may suggest the need for giving some experienced reading support to brand-new teachers.

Eighth, the oft-repeated finding that the characteristics of teachers that are explicitly rewarded—experience, extra credits of education, and degrees—are not associated with student learning is further confirmed in this study. If student learning is a school system's main objective, then some rewards based on student achievement seem appropriate.

Ninth, the policy implications from the findings on different characteristics of reading instruction are also clear: The more time spent on independent reading, the more learning there is; the enthusiasm of the teacher for the program is beneficial; the linguistic basal approach is associated with more learning growth than any of the alternatives currently used in Philadelphia; and when the teacher has more direct contact in teaching reading (that is, when the teacher uses few aides and deals with more students simultaneously, leaving fewer unattended), students learn more. Many standard approaches used in the training and development of reading teachers showed no evidence of association with increased learning for students.

Beyond these nine specific policy implications, there are two of a general nature. First, the Philadelphia findings suggest that some reallocation of inputs is possible that would require no additional resources, but would improve the growth in reading achievement of fourth graders. The findings suggest, for example, that money would be better spent on keeping teachers with students than on the usual staff development activities that take teachers away from their classrooms.

Second, this type of rigorous evaluation procedure is a useful method for school districts to use in looking at their educational processes. The technology described in this study is used in many other disciplines, including sociology, history, and psychology, but it has seldom been used in educational inquiry and rarely by individual school districts. It is a technology that can help public sector agencies in the way that price system discipline helps the private sector. Systems analysis is the public sector's efficiency tool.

We are now in an era of scarcity and restraint, and the difficulties of achieving efficiency in the public sector cannot be disguised by constantly rising levels of prosperity. Genuine appraisal of aspects of the educational

42

process needs a combination of general wisdom and modern assessment technology.

References

Christ, C. F. *Econometric Models and Methods.* New York: Wiley, 1966.

Gourman, J. *The Gourman Report.* Phoenix, Ariz.: Continuing Education Institute, 1967.

Summers. A. A., and Wolfe, B. L. *Equality of Educational Opportunity Quantified: A Production Function Approach.* Philadelphia: Federal Reserve Bank of Philadelphia, 1974.

Summers, A. A., and Wolfe, B. L. "Which School Resources Help Learning? Efficiency and Equity in Philadelphia Public Schools." *Federal Reserve Bank of Philadelphia Business Review,* 1975, *4,* 4–28.

Summers, A. A., and Wolfe, B. L. "Do Schools Make a Difference?" *American Economic Review,* 1977, *67* (4), 639–652.

Summers, A. A., and Wolfe, B. L. "Estimating Household Income from Location." *Journal of the American Statistical Association,* 1978, *73* (362), 288–292.

Theil, H. *Principles of Econometrics.* New York: Wiley, 1971.

Anita A. Summers is professor and associate chairperson of public management in the Wharton School of the University of Pennsylvania.

Mark J. Raivetz is research associate for desegregation evaluation for the School District of Philadelphia.

*This chapter examines the effect of individual, household,
and community characteristics on educational attainment and
other individual characteristics on the numeracy and literacy
of adults in rural Thailand.*

Educational Attainment and Achievement in Rural Thailand

Susan H. Cochrane
Dean T. Jamison

Modernization of developing nations always includes the spread of education,
but factors influencing the rate and consequences of its spread remain poorly
understood. Data recently available from rural Thailand allow us to examine
the effect of access to schools on educational attainment and its effect on cognitive achievement. Although our emphasis in this chapter is on results from
Thailand, some of what has been learned may be transferable to other developing nations, particularly if the findings appear to be common to several
countries. In this chapter, the factors determining educational attainment
(years of schooling completed) will be examined for children and adults, and
then the determinants of two dimensions of cognitive achievement, literacy
and numeracy, for those over age fifteen will be explored. Factors influencing

The authors thank Anita Summers, Erwin Chou, and Kowit Pravalpruk for
their helpful comments and Kalpana Mehra for her hard work and insights in the preparation of this paper. They are also indebted to Dr. Manu Seetisarn and Mr. Pichit
Thani of the Faculty of Agriculture, Chiang Mai University, for their collaboration on
data collection.

A. Summers (Ed.). *New Directions for Testing and Measurement: Productivity Assessment in Education,* no. 15.
San Francisco: Jossey-Bass, September 1982.

43

current participation in schooling of those who are of school age are pertinent to this analysis; we shall examine them briefly here.

In assessing education's spread in rural Thailand, our analysis spans three generations. The literacy of the parents of the household heads in our sample is postulated to affect both their educational participation and their educational attainment. These variables, and others (including proximity to schools), are then postulated to affect the educational participation and attainment of the children of the household heads. Before turning to these points, however, we will provide a brief account of the educational context in Thailand.

Historical Perspective

Modernization of Thai society has been profoundly shaped by the introduction of formal education during the reign of King Chulalongkorn (1868-1910). In the early years, this concern was restricted to the elite, but in 1906 the purposes of mass education were beginning to be articulated. As Wyatt has shown (1975), universal education began to be seriously pursued by 1909, and 4,000 state schools had been established by 1921. In that year, education was made compulsory for all children between the ages of seven and fourteen, but it was some time before facilities were available to provide even lower primary education to all children. The Economic and Social Commission for Asia and the Pacific (ESCAP) monograph on Thailand (Economic and Social Commission for Asia and the Pacific, 1976) provides details of this expansion. By the mid 1960s, more than 50 percent of those over age fifteen had four or more years of schooling, and by 1970 adult literacy attained 70 percent.

Despite this remarkable achievement, important regional inequalities remain, particularly in access to upper primary education (five to seven years). In the sample area used in the present study, for example, all villages had a lower primary school within two kilometers in 1972-73, but access to upper primary school was much more limited; some potential students would have had to travel fifteen kilometers to reach an upper primary school. In 1978, the old four-year (lower) and three-year (upper) primary school system cycles were reorganized as two three-year cycles, and the availability of upper primary schools was increased. In fourteen of the seventeen villages in our sample for which we have data, upper secondary schools were closer to the village in 1978 than they were in 1972-73.

For the sample used here, there has been a gradual but substantial increase in educational attainment over time. Males over fifty years of age have an average of two years of school, and females have an average of one year.

For those who are now in the fifteen- to twenty-five-year-old age bracket, the averages are 6.0 and 5.5, respectively. At all ages, females have about a half-year less schooling than males do. The determinants of educational participation and attainment among those of school age (five to twenty-five) and of those beyond normal school age (twenty-five to sixty) will be examined in the next section of this chapter. The consequences of school attainment for the achievement of literacy and numeracy will be reviewed in the following section.

Determinants of Educational Participation and Attainment

Factors Influencing School Attendance. A number of authors have analyzed investment in the education of children in developing countries as an economic decision. Their analyses have been reviewed by Birdsall and Cochrane (forthcoming). Education is an investment in human capital, and decisions depend on the costs and benefits of such investment as well as on household preferences. The costs of education depend on both the direct costs of education and the value of foregone child labor (and perhaps foregone leisure of children, depending on the family utility function). The benefits to education include (but are far from limited to) the greater potential earnings for those who have more education. The benefits also include the consumption value of education.

It is natural to expect that, as the costs of education increase, both the level of participation of children in school and the levels of educational attainment will decrease. In this sample, the direct costs of schooling include the costs of books and uniforms. These costs can vary slightly across households, but the variation is likely to be small. The major variation in the cost of education probably arises from variations in opportunity costs of the child's time. These costs include the loss of labor (or leisure) for the time that the child spends in school and the travel time to school, which we measure by the distance to school. In this study, these two costs have been measured at the community level. At the household level, the need for child labor depends on land ownership and the presence of younger siblings who need childcare.

The benefits to schooling depend on labor market conditions that can vary somewhat between villages. They also depend on the ability of individual children to capitalize on schooling. This ability is reflected in a measure of innate ability, which has been collected for all household members fourteen years of age and older. The return to schooling can depend on the sex of the child as well as on the child's ability.

Parental ability and schooling can increase the parents' educational aspirations for their children as well as affect the environment within the home that makes education less costly or more rewarding. These environmental factors include the presence of reading material and the ability of parents to help with homework. The household's demand for schooling depends on income and preferences as well as on the costs and benefits of education.

In analyzing the determinants of schooling, we split the sample into three groups: those between the ages of five and fourteen, some of whom are still attending school; those between the ages of fourteen and twenty-five, most of whom have completed school, but some of whom are making important investments beyond the normal level; and those between the ages of twenty-five and sixty, whose educational decisions were made at some time in the past. The data available on these three groups vary substantially, and the analysis will therefore vary. The educational participation and achievement of those aged five to twenty-five show little variation by sex. After age ten, educational participation drops off rapidly, but average achievement continues to increase until the late teens. We shall study the determinants of achievement, allowing the considerations just stated to guide our analysis. Before examining the empirical results, however, it is necessary to discuss the data used.

The Data. The survey described here is based on a random sample of about 400 farm households in twenty-two villages of the Chiang Mai Valley in Thailand. A parallel survey was carried out in the Nepal Terai (Jamison and Lockheed, 1981). The data analyzed in this chapter come from several different sections of the survey. Definitions of variables and their means and standard deviations are shown in Table 1.

For children between the ages of five and thirteen, data on their educational attainment and current enrollment status were obtained from the household roster. Household data are also available on land ownership, and the number of younger children can be learned from other portions of the questionnaire. Village-level data on access to schools are available, and the proportion of children between the ages of ten and fourteen working in each village has been aggregated from household rosters. This data set on individuals is unique for the extensive information on parents that it contains. Such information includes not only the parents' own education but measures of their innate intellectual ability and of their educational aspirations for their sons and daughters.

For individuals fourteen and older, data on roster information measures of their own schooling, parents' literacy status, and their own intellectual ability, literacy, and numeracy were gathered. In addition, for many of those between fourteen and twenty-five, data on their parents' educational attainment and abilities were available. Thus, for many of those in the five- to twenty-five-year-old age bracket, data were available not only on their own educational attainment but on that of their parents and grandparents.

The measures of intellectual ability, literacy, and numeracy need some

Table 1. Variable Definitions and Distribution for Various Data Sets

Variable Name	Definition	Mean	Standard deviation	n
Children 5–13				
INSCH	If child in school = 1, otherwise zero	0.74	0.44	289
YRSSCH	Years of school completed	3.70	1.93	289
AGE	Age	10.67	2.36	289
MSCHYRS	Years of school completed by person's mother	3.20	1.74	289
FSCHYRS	Years of school completed by person's father	3.43	1.63	289
MRAVSC	Mother's Ravens Score	16.43	4.84	289
FRAVSC	Father's Ravens Score	19.72	5.78	289
MDEC	Mothers' Desired Education for the Individual	8.66	4.11	289
FDEC	Father's Desired Education for the Individual	9.87	4.08	289
MDES	Mother's Desired Education for Sons	9.13	4.25	426
FDES	Father's Desired Education for Sons	10.12	4.29	386
MDED	Mother's Desired Education for Daughters	8.60	4.03	429
FDED	Father's Desired Education for Daughters	9.73	4.28	388
LAND78	Household Land Ownership 1978	5.69	7.62	289
CUNDR5	Number of Children under 6	0.24	0.49	289
PCW10-14	Proportion of children 10-14 working in village	0.23	0.13	289
LDRIMD78	Distance to lower primary school 1978	0.47	0.67	289
UPRIMD78	Distance to upper primary school 1978	2.39	3.83	289
SEX	Male = 1; female = 0	0.52	0.50	289
MADEC	Mother's desired add'l education for children	4.96	4.28	289
FADEC	Father's desired add'l education for children	6.17	4.23	289
ROADD	Distance to main road	3.27	3.34	289
AVWATER	Water availability index	0.76	0.26	289
Individuals 14–25				
INSCH	If individual is in school=1, otherwise zero	0.15	0.36	347
YRSSCH	School years completed	5.61	2.42	345
AGE	Age	18.54	2.98	345
MSCHYRS	Years of school completed by person's mother	2.63	1.93	345
FSCHYRS	Years of school completed by person's father	3.23	1.80	345
RAVSC	Individual's Ravens score	23.01	6.31	345
MRAVSC	Mother's Ravens score	16.10	4.60	345
FRAVSC	Father's Ravens Score	19.33	5.64	345
MDEC	Mother's desired education for the individual	8.52	4.19	345
FDEC	Father's desired education for the individual	9.80	4.38	345

Table 1. Variable Definitions and Distribution for Various Data Sets *(continued)*

Variable Name	Variable Definition	Mean	Standard deviation	n
Individuals 14–25 (continued)				
MDES	Mother's desired education for sons	8.73	4.28	181
FDES	Father's desired education for sons	10.10	4.46	181
MDED	Mother's desired education for daughters	8.29	4.08	164
FDED	Father's desired eduation for daughters	9.48	4.29	164
OLAND73	Land-owned by household in 1973	5.69	6.42	345
CUNDR13	Children in household under 14	1.14	1.01	345
LPRIMD72	Distance to lower primary school in 1972	0.41	0.65	345
UPRIMD72	Distnce to upper primary school in 1972	6.53	3.45	345
SEX	Males = 1, females = 0	0.52	0.50	345
AVWATER	Water availability index	0.74	0.23	345
Individuals 14–60				
AGE	Age	33.37	14.53	1205
SCHYRS	School years completed	4.29	2.53	1205
RAVSC	Score on Ravens Color Progressive Matrix	20.43	6.57	1205
LITSC	Score on a test of reading and writing	12.25	5.57	1205
NUMSC	Score on a test of arithmetic ability(NUMA+NUMB)	9.35	2.19	1230
NUMA	Score on a test of addition and subtraction	3.61	0.75	1230
NUMB	Score on a test of multiplication and division	5.71	1.77	1242
SEX	Males = 1, females = 0	0.49	0.50	1274
Males 25–60				
AGE	Age	44.09	9.47	334
RAVSC	Ravens score	19.75	6.12	334
MLIT	Mother's literacy status, 1=yes, 2=no	1.86	0.35	334
FLIT	Father's literacy status, 1=yes, 2=no	1.65	0.48	334
YPLACE	Location when growing up	0.06	0.24	334
PRIMVA	School was available in village when he was a child	0.23	0.42	334
Females 25–60				
AGE	Age	42.43	9.97	351
RAVSC	Ravens score	16.85	5.28	351
MLIT	Mother's literacy status, 1=yes, no=2	1.85	0.36	351
FLIT	Father's literacy status, 1=yes, no=2	1.62	0.49	351
YPLACE	Location when growing up	0.04	0.19	351
PRIMVA	School was available in village when she was a child	0.23	0.42	351

further explanation. To measure innate ability, Ravens's Coloured Progressive Matrix (Ravens, 1956) was used. This is an inferential test that is not language dependent and that does not depend on schooling per se; it is intended to be a measure (though imperfect) of natural intellectual endowment. This test has been used in a wide variety of cultures. The mean score was 20.43 for the sample; the maximum score was 36.

Tests of reading and writing were used to measure literacy. Scores on these tests have been aggregated. A test of comprehension was also given, but results were not used in the analysis presented here, because the subject matter used for the test was widely known. The mean score for reading and writing was 12.25; the maximum was 16.

To measure numeracy, individuals were asked four questions that required addition or subtraction and nine that required multiplication or division. On the average, 3.6 of the first four questions and 5.7 of the last nine questions were answered correctly.

Evidence on Determinants of Educational Attainment. Multiple regression was used to analyze the determinants of educational attainment. The results for children aged five to thirteen, displayed in Table 2, show that (other than age) the aspirations of father and mother for the child's schooling are the most significant factors affecting attainment for boys. Access to upper primary schooling is a significant constraint on the participation of boys and girls. For girls, attainment increases as ownership of land by the family increases. Father's—but not mother's—aspirations for their daughter's schooling and father's innate ability have positive effects on attainment. While there is some difference in the factors that are significant for boys and girls, there is no significant difference in the level of attainment of boys and girls after controlling for other factors. Measures of the benefits of educating children include the presence of younger children in the household, water availability for year-round cropping, and proportion of children aged ten to fourteen working in the village; all are insignificant. Thus, aspirations of parents and access to upper primary school proved the most significant factors.

To explore the role of access more fully, the effect of school availability five years ago on the attainment of those aged fourteen to twenty-five can be analyzed. Another way of exploring the impact of access on achievement is by examining the current enrollment of children in school and its relationship to access. Both of these will be discussed here.

The same factors that affect the educational attainment of young adults should affect the attainment of younger children, except that age may play a lesser role, since most children in the sample complete school prior to age fourteen. Determinants of schooling can be more fully analyzed with this age group, because measures of their innate ability are available.

Table 2. The Determinants of Years of School Completed
for Those 5-13 Years

	Pooled	Males	Females
Constant	−5.057	−6.008	−4.663
AGE	0.821***	0.738**	0.966**
	(3.10)	(2.46)	(2.02)
AGESQ	−0.011	−0.004	−0.020
	(0.79)	(0.26)	(0.83)
MDEC	0.044**	0.076***	0.010
	(2.15)	(3.34)	(0.28)
FDEC	0.055***	0.056**	0.055*
	(2.67)	(2.33)	(1.67)
MSCHYRS	0.084*	0.109*	0.103
	(1.84)	(1.89)	(1.46)
FSCHYRS	−0.035	−0.071	0.025
	(0.68)	(1.19)	(0.31)
MRAVSC	−0.011	0.003	−0.031
	(0.61)	(0.15)	(1.07)
FRAVSC	0.017	0.033*	−
	(1.24)	(1.94)	−
PCW10-14	−	0.255	−0.615
	−	(0.37)	(0.58)
CUNDR5	−0.065	0.156	−0.218
	(0.41)	(0.84)	(0.83)
LAND78	0.018*	0.004	0.036**
	(1.75)	(0.33)	(2.08)
LPRIMD78	0.050	−0.187	0.250
	(0.43)	(1.29)	(1.40)
UPRIMD78	−0.064***	−0.068**	−0.064*
	(3.11)	(2.51)	(1.85)
AVWATER	0.203	0.413	−
	(0.68)	(1.10)	−
SEX	−0.170	−	−
	(1.16)	−	−
R^2	0.61	0.72	0.51
N	289	149	140

*** Significant at 1%; ** Significant at 5%; * Significant at 10%.

Note: Entries in the table are the estimated regression coefficients in
a linear regression; the numbers in parentheses below the coefficients are t-values.

Empirical investigation shows that ability is consistently the most important factor — other than age — that affects schooling for those aged fourteen
to twenty-five, as shown in Table 3. Ability is followed in importance by the

Table 3. Determinants of Schooling Among Young Adults (14-25)

	Pooled	Males	Females
Constant	-1.279	-11.886	6.512
AGE	0.367	1.408**	-0.377
	(0.87)	(2.15)	(0.68)
AGESQ	-0.012	-0.039**	0.007
	(1.14)	(2.31)	(0.47)
RAVSC	0.119***	0.165***	0.091***
	(6.50)	(5.65)	(3.86)
MDEC	0.137***	0.140***	0.116***
	(4.83)	(3.48)	(2.83)
FDEC	0.079***	0.046	0.117***
	(3.04)	(1.26)	(3.23)
MSCHYRS	-0.009	-0.059	0.054
	(0.14)	(0.65)	(0.61)
FSCHYRS	0.101	0.077	0.124
	(1.50)	(0.78)	(1.33)
MRAVSC	-.0.033	-0.022	-0.031
	(1.21)	(0.53)	(0.63)
FRAVSC	0.025	0.028	0.019
	(1.20)	(0.97)	(0.90)
PCW10-14	-1.010	-0.549	-1.277
	(1.20)	(0.43)	(1.14)
CUNDR13	-0.353***	-0.542***	-0.291**
	(3.23)	(3.24)	(2.07)
OLAND73	0.048***	0.074***	-
	(2.73)	(3.04)	-
LPRIMD72	-0.451**	-0.556*	-0.332
	(2.46)	(1.94)	(1.39)
UPRIMD72	-0.067*	-0.070	-0.074
	(1.89)	(1.34)	(1.50)
AVWATER	0.505	0.923	0.194
	(1.06)	(1.24)	(0.31)
SEX	0.262	-	-
	(1.24)	-	-
$\bar{R}^2$	0.38	0.38	0.38
N	345	181	164

*** Significant at 1%; ** Significant at 5%; * Significant at 10%.

Note: Entries in the table are the estimated regression coefficients in a linear regression; the numbers in parentheses below the coefficients are t-values.

educational aspirations of mothers for their children. Fathers' educational aspirations for sons is not significant, but it is significant for daughters. Parental education and ability are generally insignificant, since they probably operate by increasing parental aspirations. The availability of land has a positive effect on schooling of sons but not on that of daughters. The presence of children under age thirteen has a negative effect on the attainment of sons and daughters.

Most interesting from a policy perspective, the availability of upper and lower primary schools in 1972 has a generally significant effect. This effect is much stronger and more consistent than the parallel effect in the achievement of all those between the ages of five and thirteen. This probably results from the fact that there were fewer schools in the area in 1972 and that travel distances were greater as a result.

There has been a secular increase in the schooling of males and females in the sample studied. There are relatively few data, however, on the factors affecting educational decisions at the time they were made for those over age twenty-five. There are data, however, on their parents' education, their own ability, the place where they grew up, and whether there was a primary or secondary school in their village of residence when they were of school age. Table 4 shows the effect of these factors on the school attainment of adults aged twenty-five to sixty.

The measure of innate ability has a strong positive effect on school

Table 4. Determinants of Educational Attainment in Adults (25–60)

	Males	Females
Constant	2.94	-1.57
AGE	0.085	0.293***
	(1.09)	(4.31)
AGESQ	0.001	-.004**
	(1.45)	(5.53)
RAVSC	0.072***	0.067***
	(5.05)	(4.28)
MLIT	0.654**	-
	(2.15)	-
FLIT	0.324	0.345**
	(1.55)	(2.04)
YPLACE	0.75**	-0.211
	(2.05)	(0.51)
PRIMVA	0.054	0.276
	(0.25)	(1.43)
R^2	0.17	0.35
N	334	351

*** Significant at 1%;   ** Significant at 5%;   * Significant at 10%.

Note: Entries in the table are the estimated regression coefficients in a linear regression; the numbers in parentheses below the coefficients are t-values.

attainment for both men and women. The literacy of the parent of opposite sex has a significantly positive effect for men and women. For women, age has a significant nonlinear effect. The older the woman, the less education she is likely to have. This effect levels off only at very advanced ages. The only other variable of significance is whether a man lived in a town or a city before coming to the village, which increases schooling. Our measure of the availability of a primary school in the village at the time when the adult was growing up was insignificant, but this may reflect the poor quality of data on the length of time that a school had been present in the village.

In this section, factors influencing the educational attainment of those aged five to thirteen, fourteen to twenty-five, and over twenty-five have been examined for males and females. Access to school and parental aspirations are most important for the two younger groups. Innate ability is, however, the most significant factor for those in the fourteen- to twenty-five year bracket. For the oldest individuals, who are no longer likely to be investing in additional years of school, innate ability and their parents' education level are the most consistent factors. For those who are still of an age to increase their schooling, it is important to study the determinants of current enrollment in school, and to that we now turn.

Evidence on Determinants of Educational Participation. Attainment is the result of a series of decisions to enroll in school and to remain in school. One problem in investigating the factors that determine attainment is that the variables measured may not always be relevant to the time period in which the decision was made. This is true of family variables, such as income level or number of dependent children, and of village variables such as the availability of employment opportunities for children and the availability of schools. To get a more accurate picture of the factors affecting the sequences of decisions that determine ultimate educational attainment, we will examine determinants of current participation in school.

Factors assumed to influence current participation in school include the excess demand for education by mothers and fathers (that is, aspiration minus achievement), the access to lower and upper primary schools, and the individual's age. Table 5 shows that the factors affecting participation differ by age group and also by sex for the youngest group. Age has the expected nonlinear effect for the youngest group, and the males in this group are more likely to attend school than the girls are. The parents' demand for additional schooling for their children has a significant effect on the participation of young girls but no effect on the participation of young males or older children. Access to upper primary school is clearly a significant constraint on the schooling of young males but — rather surprisingly — not for females or for older males or females.

Table 5. Factors Influencing Educational Participation in Thailand

	Individuals Aged 5-13			Individuals Aged 14-25		
	Pooled	Male	Female	Pooled	Male	Female
Constant	−9.21	−8.92	−10.04	5.49	4.85	1.99
RAVSC	−	−	−	0.16***	0.14***	0.21***
	−	−	−	(6.33)	(4.48)	(4.14)
AGE	2.32***	2.33***	2.52***	−0.83*	−0.70	−0.48
	(6.61)	(4.69)	(4.61)	(1.83)	(1.28)	(0.33)
AGESQ	−0.12***	−0.12***	−0.13***	0.02	0.01	0.00
	(6.78)	(4.76)	(4.79)	(1.31)	(0.95)	(0.07)
MADEC	0.03	−0.00	0.08**	−0.02	−0.02	−0.02
	(1.18)	(0.11)	(2.13)	(0.66)	(0.42)	(0.25)
FADEC	0.05**	0.05	0.04	0.02	0.01	0.04
	(2.03)	(1.38)	(1.06)	(0.68)	(0.18)	(0.63)
LAND78	−0.01	−0.01	−0.00	−0.00	0.01	−0.02
	(0.65)	(0.42)	(0.13)	(0.00)	(0.65)	(0.74)
CUNDR5 or	−0.05	0.00	−0.12	−0.36***	−0.32*	−0.45**
CUNDR13	(0.26)	(0.01)	(0.42)	(2.87)	(1.93)	(2.17)
ROADD	0.03	0.06	0.01	0.00	0.01	−0.00
	(1.06)	(1.30)	(0.29)	(0.04)	(0.21)	(0.10)
LPRIMD78	0.02	−0.19	0.24	0.14	0.17	0.12
	(0.17)	(0.90)	(1.29)	(0.76)	(0.70)	(0.38)
UPRIMD78	−0.04	−0.05	−0.02	−0.05	−0.05	−0.07
	(1.61)	(1.49)	(0.60)	(1.01)	(0.75)	(0.62)
AVWATER	−0.75	−0.40	−1.09	−0.89	−1.07	−0.59
	(1.55)	(0.56)	(1.52)	(1.51)	(1.31)	(0.68)
SEX	0.41**	−	−	0.24	−	−
	(2.20)	−	−	(1.10)	−	−
R^2	0.23	0.25	0.26	0.32	0.27	0.41
N	289	149	140	347	182	165

*** Significant at 1%; ** Significant at 5%; * Significant at 10%.

Note: The dependent variable in the analyses reported in this table takes the value '1' if the child is currently enrolled in school and '0' otherwise; hence it is inappropriate to analyze the data using standard regression models that assume a continuous dependent variable. We have used instead a probit model, which can be interpreted as modelling the probability that the dependent variable take on the value '1'; entries in the table measure the strength of the influence of the indicated independent variable on this probability. Numbers in parenthesis below the entries are analogous to t-values and provide a measure of the statistical significance of the influence of the independent variable.

For children older than age thirteen (who should have completed primary school), only age and ability affect participation. If the measure of ability used here does in fact reflect innate ability, not the effects of schooling, then the results on participation of those aged fourteen to twenty-five is reassuring. That is, they are the more able who continue in school, not those who have wealthy parents. Neither sex nor distance from the main road (the best measure that we have of distance to secondary schools) is a significant constraint on participation. If the ability score is left out, distance to upper primary schools has a significantly negative effect on participation of sons but not of daughters.

Although the desired additional achievement of children is not a binding constraint in most cases in this sample, educational aspirations are highly significant in explaining attainment. Therefore, it is important to examine its determinants. Table 6 shows the results of this examination. Parental education and innate ability are the most significant factors explaining aspirations, and these effects are perfectly consistent for fathers and mothers, sons and daughters. Thus, it appears that the main effect of parents' educational background on attainment is through aspirations.

The analysis just described showed that parental aspirations for their children's education was highly significant in explaining the years of school completed by children. Parents' education, however, had little direct effect; apparently, it operated through parental aspirations. This insight is useful, but it does not answer one of the basic questions about education: How significant is parents' education in determining the level of education of their children? To answer this question, the analysis of years of school completed was redone, using only parent's education and omitting both parental aspirations and parental ability. The analysis of adult schooling showed that the literacy of the opposite-sex parent was highly significant in determining the years of

Table 6. Determinants of Educational Aspirations for Children

	Fathers		Mothers	
	DES	DED	DES	DED
Constant	6.82	6.63	6.30	5.93
SCHYRS 0.45***	0.42***	0.429***	0.375***	
(4.01)	(3.86)	(4.07)	(3.75)	
RAVSC 0.102***	0.130***	0.087**	0.104***	
(2.71)	(3.49)	(2.16)	(2.71)	
CUNDR5 0.422	0.412	−0.100	−0.318	
(0.95)	(0.95)	(0.25)	(0.83)	
PCW10–14	−1.526	−2.089	−4.228***	−3.797***
(1.02)	(1.43)	(3.03)	(2.87)	
LAND78 0.011	0.006	0.014	0.017	
(0.52)	(0.28)	(0.74)	(0.95)	
AVWATER	−	−0.673	1.425*	0.972
−	(0.80)	(1.90)	(1.36)	
$\bar{R}^2$ 0.08	0.10	0.09	0.09	
N 386	388	426	429	

*** Significant at 1%; ** Significant at 5%; * Significant at 10%.

Note: Entries in the table are the estimated regression coefficients in a linear regression; the numbers in parentheses below the coefficients are t-values.

school completed. For those aged five to thirteen, mother's education is significant for both boys and girls. For those aged fourteen to twenty-five, father's education is significant only for girls, and mother's education is not significant. In both cases, for those aged fourteen to twenty-five, the individual's innate ability is the most important factor affecting attainment. This implies that ability is perhaps more important than social selectivity in this area.

The costs and benefits of education as measured by landownership and the presence of children under age five are not significant, but the availability of water for year-round farming and the proportion of children aged ten to fourteen in the village who are working have significantly positive and negative effects, respectively, on aspirations of mothers but not of fathers. Access to lower primary school has a marginal effect on the aspirations of fathers.

Literacy and Numeracy Consequences of Educational Attainment

Education has been hypothesized to affect behavior in many ways. As a recent *World Development Report* (World Bank, 1980) argues, "Schooling imparts specific knowledge and develops general reasoning skills (its cognitive effects); it also induces changes in beliefs and values and in attitudes toward work and society (noncognitive effects). The relative importance of these is much debated but poorly understood; both are extremely important" (World Bank, 1980, p. 47).

Earlier in this chapter, the effects of parents' education on their aspirations for the educational achievement of their children were examined. The effects of education on attitudes toward and use of contraception have been documented elsewhere (Cochrane and Nandwani, 1982). In this section, the effect of education on the cognitive outcomes—literacy and numeracy—of those aged fourteen to sixty will be assessed. Previous studies of schooling's effects on basic cognitive skills have been reviewed by Harnqvist (1977) and by Sheffield (no date).

The effect of education is significant for both numeracy and for literacy, but in both cases the effect of education differs with the level of schooling. Table 7 shows the basic results. For literacy, the first three years of schooling have a significant effect, but completion of four years has a significantly greater effect. Higher levels of schooling have very little additional effect on improving literacy scores on the fairly simple literacy tests used in this study. Thus, there does appear to be something close to a literacy threshold effect of schooling at four years—complete lower primary.

The effect of schooling on numeracy varies by sex. For women, each increment in level increases numeracy significantly, but for males only the

Table 7. Nonlinear Effects of Education on Cognitive Outcomes

	Literacy			Numeracy		
	Pooled	Males	Females	Pooled	Males	Females
Constant	-1.23	-2.73	0.624	3.56	3.66	3.83
AGE	-.012	0.057	-0.064	0.102***	0.152***	0.049
	(0.30)	(1.04)	(1.15)	(3.67)	(4.00)	(1.19)
AGESQ	0.0001	-0.0006	-0.0003	-0.001***	-0.002***	-0.0005
	(0.10)	(0.81)	(0.48)	(3.03)	(3.44)	(0.83)
S1(1-3 yrs)a/	5.51***	6.10***	4.84***	0.546*	-0.633	1.323***
	(14.96)	(10.54)	(9.87)	(1.95)	(1.40)	(3.56)
S2(4 yrs)	13.51***	13.71***	13.04***	1.34***	0.668*	1.615***
	(44.53)	(28.14)	(32.01)	(5.50)	(1.67)	(4.97)
S3 (5-6 yrs)	13.08***	13.33***	12.63***	1.23***	0.606	1.51***
	(35.32)	(24.75)	(22.52)	(4.44)	(1.40)	(3.60)
S4 (7+ yrs)	13.83***	14.42***	12.98***	2.12***	1.71***	2.07***
	(34.47)	(24.30)	(22.82)	(6.93)	(3.66)	(4.83)
RAVSC	0.116***	0.108***	0.111***	0.135***	0.115***	0.152***
(8.35)	(5.66)	(5.52)	(13.79)	(8.54)	(10.64)	
SEX	0.018	-		-0.152	-	-
	(0.11)	-		(1.34)	-	-
R^2	0.78	0.71	0.82	0.25	0.23	0.28
N	1205	694	611	1230	616	614

*** Significant at 1%; ** Significant at 5%; * Significant at 10%.

a/ The variables S1, S2, S3 and S4 are ´0´ - ´1´ indicator variables that take on the value ´1´ if the individual has completed the number of years of education in the indicated interval. Individuals who have not completed any schooling would have values of ´0´ for all 4 of these variables, and the coefficients of these variables show how many more points on the indicated test an individual with the indicated number of years of schooling would have in comparison to an individual with no schooling. A male in group S2, for example, would be expected to score 13.7 points higher on the literacy test than a male with no schooling.

Note: Entries in the table are the estimated regression coefficients in a linear regression; the numbers in parentheses below the coefficients are t-values.

completion of seven years of schooling has more than a marginal effect. For males, it appears that numeracy is more closely related to age than to schooling. Numeracy generally increases with age. This may result from learning by doing in day-to-day work. For both males and females, innate ability is positively related to literacy and numeracy.

These results are useful in evaluating the direct consequences of schooling. They are also useful for evaluating, in other studies that use this data set, how much of the effect that education has on economic performance on the farm and in off-farm employment arises from the cognitive consequences of schooling and how much to other outcomes of the educational process.

Summary and Policy Conclusions

The determinants of educational participation and attainment vary in our sample between males and females and between younger and older children. Current participation in school is determined exclusively by age and innate ability among those aged fourteen to twenty-five. This is reasuring if our measure of innate ability indicates that the more able remain in school. Among younger children, the main constraint on participation for boys is access to upper primary school, while for girls it is mother's desire for additional education for girls. This sex difference is rather surprising and implies that increased access alone may not increase participation for girls.

For attainment, access to upper primary school appears to have been significant for young boys and girls, and access to both upper and lower primary school five years ago was a constraint on the attainment of older boys but not of girls. For older girls, mother's desire for daughter's education is the most significant factor. This seems to reinforce the findings on current enrollment.

The effect of other variables, such as family landownership, water availability, presence of younger children, and child employment in the village, all vary substantially from group to group. Wealth as measured by landownership and water availability have positive effects when they are significant. This implies that the income effect of these factors increases the demand for schooling more than these factors increase the demand for child labor. The presence of younger children in the household significantly reduces the attainment of boys and girls aged fourteen to twenty-five, but not of younger children. Thus, the economic model provides a useful way of studying the determinants of schooling. It is particularly interesting that the binding constraints vary between males and females in a society where there is such a high degree of equity in education.

References

Birdsall, N., and Cochrane, S. H. "Education and Parental Decision Making: A Two-Generation Approach." In L. Anderson and D. Windham (Eds.), *Education and Development.* Lexington, Mass.: Lexington Press, forthcoming.

Cochrane, S. H., and Nandwani, K. *The Determinants of Fertility in Twenty-Two Villages of Northern Thailand.* Discussion Paper No. 81–59. Washington, D.C.: Population and Human Resources Division, World Bank, 1981.

Economic and Social Commission for Asia and the Pacific. *Country Monograph Series No. 3: Population of Thailand.* Bangkok: United Nations, 1976.

Harnqvist, K. "Enduring Effects of Schooling: A Neglected Area in Educational Research." *Educational Researcher,* 1977, *6* (10), 5–11.

Jamison, D. T., and Lockheed, M. E. *Participation in Schooling: Determinants and Learning Outcomes in Nepal.* Washington, D.C.: Population and Human Resources Division, World Bank, 1981.

Ravens, J. C. *Guide to Using the Coloured Progressive Matrices.* London: Lewis, 1956.

Sheffield, J. R. "Retention of Literacy and Basic Skills: A Review of the Literature." Paper prepared for the Education Department, World Bank, no date.

World Bank. *World Development Report, 1980.* Washington, D.C.: World Bank, 1980.

Wyatt, D. K. "Education and the Modernization of Thai Society." In A. W. Skinner and A. T. Kirsch (Eds.), *Change and Persistence in Thai Society.* Ithaca, N.Y.: Cornell University Press, 1975.

Susan H. Cochrane joined the Population and Human Resources Division of the World Bank as Brookings Policy Fellow in 1976. She has published widely in the field of population economics as well as in development economics.

Dean T. Jamison joined the Population and Human Resources Division of the World Bank in 1976 and is now project officer in its Population, Health, and Nutrition Department. He has published widely in the economics of education as well as in economic theory.

*Increased schooling is being undertaken in the developing countries
in order to increase productivity and to affect other socioeconomic
characteristics, such as health and family formation. Detailed study
of one developing country, Nicaragua, indicates that schooling productivity
seems often to be misunderstood and that considerable overstatements
in certain respects and substantial underestimates in others are the result.*

Is Schooling Productivity in Developing Countries Often Misunderstood?

Barbara L. Wolfe
Jere R. Behrman

Formal education in the form of schooling is widely believed to be a very important factor in the pursuit of various growth and income distribution goals in developing economies. In its annual *World Development Report,* for example, the World Bank (1980, 1981) places considerable emphasis on the roles of in-

This chapter reports findings from a survey and research project investigating the social, economic, and demographic roles of women in the developing country of Nicaragua. Funding for 1977–1978 was provided by the Population and Development Policy Research Program, sponsored jointly by the Ford and Rockefeller Foundations. Further funding was provided for 1977–1981 by Negotiated Contract AID/otr-C 1571 from the Agency for International Development and for 1980–1983 by Grant SES-8025356 from the National Science Foundation. Behrman also was a Guggenheim Fellow for part of the 1979–1980 academic year and a Compton Foundation Fellow for part of 1980–1981. The authors would like to thank, but not to implicate, the editor of this volume, the funding agencies, and their coprincipal investigators, research associates, and colleagues. Wolfe and Behrman share equal responsibility for this chapter.

A. Summers (Ed.). *New Directions for Testing and Measurement: Productivity Assessment in Education,* no. 15.
San Francisco: Jossey-Bass, September 1982.

creased schooling in expanding personal income and output, satisfying basic needs, limiting population growth, and improving distribution of command over resources for the poor in general, as well as for particular target groups, such as women or landless rural laborers. Underlying these emphases are widespread hypotheses regarding the high productivity of schooling. Consequently, the developing countries as a group have considerably expanded the resources devoted to schooling. Current public expenditures on schooling in these countries are estimated by the World Bank to be about $40 billion per year, which is a considerable sum.

But, the extent of increased productivity due to schooling depends on the definition of product and on the viewpoint that is taken. For instance, if fertility is reduced because schooling induces taste changes favoring consumption of goods, services, and leisure over having children, there may be social productivity gains—that is, resources saved because fewer children mean lowered public costs for schooling—but no private productivity gains, only a change in preferences for children. Moreover, measurement of schooling productivity is difficult. Empirically estimated effects of schooling may be due to increased efficiency in market production of goods and services or in household production related to raising children, general health and nutrition, and so forth. But, they may also reflect changes in personal preferences, inclusion of nonrepresentative people in the sample, or omission of variables related to family background (for example, genetic endowments or quality of schooling), each of which has different welfare and policy implications. Furthermore, some gains from the point of view of individuals are not gains for society, since they only involve redistribution of products among members of society, not additions to the total social product. Finally, some apparent effects estimated from cross section studies do not necessarily mean that the same effects will prevail if schooling is increased for many members of society. For example, the productivity returns for highly schooled individuals can be large in a cross section comparison, but increasing everyone's schooling over time will not necessarily have equally high returns, since the aggregate increase in skills reduces their scarcity and thus their marginal productivity.

In this chapter, we report on extensive investigations that we have undertaken on the impact of schooling in one developing country, particularly for women, as measured by a range of socioeconomic outcomes. We begin by exploring the effect of schooling on a wide range of outcomes, using individuals or households as the unit of observation. For the non–labor market outcomes, we go beyond the standard estimates by distinguishing between the impact of schooling through increasing labor market productivity (and thus the cost of time) and through other effects. Then, we consider the impact of schooling using adult sibling data so that the schooling coefficients are not contaminated by unobserved factors related to family background, such as ability and motivation. In doing so, we illustrate some of the problems in measuring schooling productivity as socioeconomic outcomes, and we conclude that frequently used approaches may misrepresent schooling productivity in developing countries by overstating some dimensions and understating others.

Socioeconomic Impacts of Schooling on Individuals and Households in a Developing Country

Data and Methods. Our empirical estimates are based on analysis of an area-stratified, random sample of about 4,000 women aged fifteen to forty-five whom we interviewed in the developing country of Nicaragua in 1977 and 1978. Because of frequent differences in the impact of schooling among geographical areas in developing countries, we disaggregate the national sample into three regions, defined by degree of urbanization: the central metropolis, which has about a quarter of the country's inhabitants and which is the economic, political, and cultural center of the nation; other urban areas, each of which has between 500 and 80,000 inhabitants and many of which are regional or local political and economic centers; and rural areas. As in many developing countries, although there have been recent large increases in the resources devoted to education, average schooling levels among current adults are much lower than in most industrialized and socialist countries. For women, the average grades of schooling completed are 5.3 years in the central metropolis, 4.9 in the other urban areas, and only 1.6 years in rural areas. For men, the average schooling figures indicate an even sharper urban-rural dichotomy, with respective values of 6.6, 6.1, and 1.3 grades completed.

We explore the impact of schooling within a multivariate context with controls for other variables in efforts to avoid biases in our estimated impacts of schooling. For example, to clarify the impact of schooling on various dimensions of household productivity, we include in the estimated relations a control for the value of time spent by the woman in market activities. Predicted earnings in paid market activities, given her characteristics, are the measure. In further efforts to avoid biases, we attempt to control for selectivity into the sample and other nonlinearities.

Table 1 summarizes the estimated direct impacts of schooling on a number of socioeconomic outcomes. The estimated impact of schooling on the three groups of socioeconomic outcomes indicated in this table is discussed first: labor market activities, household production, and other activities. Then, three implications of these estimates are considered: the use of schooling to try to alter the distribution of income, the role of tastes versus efficiency changes, and private and social welfare.

Table 1. Direct Socioeconomic Returns to Schooling in Terms of Market Outcomes, Household Productivity and Other Effects on National and Regional Levels in Nicaragua, 1977-1978

Outcomes	Nation	Central Metropolis	Other Urban	Rural
Paid Labor Market Activities				
1. Female labor force participation (probability)[a] plus sector selection:	.09	.04	.11	.04[b]
(1A) formal		.19[b]	.18	.25[c]
(1B) informal		-.07[b]	-.02[c]	.06[c]
(1C) domestic		-.15[b]	-.12[c]	
2. Female earnings (rates of return)[a]	.11(26)	.10(28)	.11(26)	.06[b](9)
(2A) formal		.13(52)	.18(61)	.03[b](5)
(2B) informal		.08[b](18)	.04[b](8)	.08[b](11)
(2C) domestic		-.07(-10)	.07[b](7)	
3. Male earnings (rates of return)[d]	.07(48)	.08(62)	.07(55)	.02[b](6)
Household Production				
4. Child mortality (probabilities)[e]	-.09	-.06[b]	-.10	-.05[b]
5. Child health and nutrition:[e]				
(5A) standardized weight	.04	.05[c]	.04[c]	.09
(5B) standardized height	.05	.05[c]	.06[c]	.10[c]
(5C) standardized bicep	.003	.002[c]	.003[c]	.01
6. Standardized household nutrient intake[f]	.05	.03	.13[c]	.06
7. Knowledge of contraceptives (probabilities)[g]	.14	.09[b]	.16[b]	.19
8. Male spouse's earnings (rates of return to woman's schooling)[d]	.05(38)	.05(40)	.06(47)	.02[b](5)
Other Effects				
9. Fertility: number of children[h]	.001	-.006	.012	.007
10. Use of modern contraceptives (probabilities)[g]	.098	.049[b]	.080[b]	.235

11. Assortive mating (male spouse's schooling)[d]	.68	.63	.76	.35
12. Migration[j]		.10	-.19	.17

a Source: Behrman and Wolfe (1981b, Tables 1, 2, 4, 6), based on control for double selectivity (see Behrman, Wolfe and Tunali, 1981) within multivariable framework with quadratic effects evaluated at appropriate sample means. The numbers in parentheses are the implied cordobas per fortnight at the sample means for the rates of return estimates. Also see Behrman and Wolfe (1982g).

b Underlying coefficient estimates are not significantly nonzero at 10% level.

c Underlying coefficient estimates are significantly nonzero at 10% level, whereas those with no notes are significantly nonzero at 5% level.

d Source: Behrman and Wolfe (1982f, Tables 1, 3), with other details as in note c. Row 3 refers to the male's schooling; Row 8 to his spouse's.

e Source: Wolfe and Behrman (1982b, Tables 3, 4, 5, 6). The weight and height measures are standardized by international age and sex-specific measures. The biceps measure is standardized by age and sex-specific averages from the sample. Generally the weight index is assumed to refer to short-run health and nutrition status and the height and bicpes ones to long-run status. Mortality refers to probit estimates of whether or not children born in the five years prior to the survey had died by the time of the survey.

f Source: Behrman and Wolfe (1982d). Also see Wolfe and Behrman (1982c). The results here are for standardized average household caloric intakes relative to international standards. The estimates for protein, vitamin A and iron are similar with, if anything, a stronger association with the woman's schooling.

g Source: Behrman and Wolfe (1982b, Tables 1 and 2 for all ages). Based on probit estimates so the effects are nonlinear, but here are evaluated at the sample means.

h Source: Behrman and Wolfe (1982a, Table 4). These are complicated nonlinear results evaluated at the sample means.

Labor Market Effects. The socioeconomic impact of schooling most emphasized by economists is its impact on labor market outcomes. It is widely believed that schooling increases the output of goods and services per worker and thus increases labor market earnings. This possibility can be considered in three stages.

First, there is the question of whether schooling increases the participation of individuals in the labor force. The standard economic model posits that an individual decides whether to participate in the labor force after comparing the returns from market versus nonmarket use of time, given his or her characteristics. The common presumption is that schooling affects market returns more strongly than it affects nonmarket returns. However, for prime-age men, we find no significant impact of schooling on labor force participation (Behrman and Wolfe, 1981a), a common result also for more industrial countries. For women, again as for more industrial countries, we find a positive significant impact of schooling on labor force participation in the urban regions. The empirical findings suggest that another grade of schooling increases market returns relative to returns from nonmarket activities, so that for a women with characteristics equal to the national averages, the probability of participating in the labor force increases by 9 percent.

Second, there is an important question in developing countries regarding the part of the labor market in which a given individual participates. Productivity generally is high in the formal sector (where individuals work with others in a firm, receive salaries, and work fixed hours) but much lower in the informal sector (where individuals work alone or with others, work irregular hours, and receive no salary and no fringe benefits), or for domestics (persons who work in others persons' homes performing household and childrearing tasks). The economic rewards also are generally highest in the formal sector, with regular employment, fringe benefits, and more machinery and equipment than in the informal sector or for domestics. The estimates in rows 1A–1C of Table 1 combine this sector selection procedure with the labor force participation decision. They indicate that this sorting among sectors is an important labor market role of schooling that is masked by the aggregate participation estimates. In the urban regions, a woman with average characteristics but with one additional grade of schooling has about a fifth higher probability of being in the generally higher-productivity and more rewarding formal sector than of being in the other two sectors or of not being in the labor force at all.

Third, as we have already noted, schooling can alter productivity in market activities and therefore earnings. The estimates in rows 2 and 3 of Table 1 suggest a significant association of schooling with earnings for both women and men in urban areas. Under the assumption that these associations do indeed reflect a productivity-increasing effect of schooling, the implied real rates of return in labor market activities (that is, the proportional change in earnings due to an additional year of schooling) range from 7 to 11 percent.

Five points about these estimates merit further emphasis. First, the magnitudes are such that investment in schooling may be reasonably attractive, but not nearly so much as indicated by the average rates of returns for developing countries of more than 20 percent cited by the World Bank (1980). The World Bank does not provide details about its estimates, so it is not possible to be sure why they are higher than ours. But, whatever the source of the difference, our results suggest that the World Bank conclusion about the high market productivity returns of schooling investments does not apply to all developing countries. Second, the World Bank (1980) also claims that the rates of return are highest for primary schooling, but our estimates again question this generalization, since they imply increasing rates of return as schooling increases, not the opposite. Third, some care must be taken in extrapolating from these cross section estimates to the effects of aggregate schooling increases, as Tobin (1973) and others have suggested. There may be high earnings returns for high schooling in such a cross section because of current scarcity of highly educated individuals. But, if schooling is increased broadly, those with much schooling will become relatively less scarce, so the earnings returns for their schooling may fall. That tendency may be offset, however, if there is also a change over time toward higher demand for more-schooled individuals due to changes in the nature of demand, as seems to have happened in most developed economies. Fourth, the sectoral estimates for women in rows 2A–2C of Table 1 suggest that aggregation masks the true nature of these returns, which are much higher in the urban formal sectors than they are elsewhere, a pattern that reinforces the point made earlier about the relatively high rewards for formal sector employment. Fifth, the patterns of estimates do not indicate sexual discrimination against women in the sense that their marginal rates of return for schooling are lower. On the contrary, the estimated marginal rates of return in terms of one's own earnings, if anything, are higher for women than they are for men. But, the overall earnings relations indicate higher average earnings for men than for women due to unobserved sex-associated factors, which may either be traits like physical strength or manual dexterity or be labor market discrimination. The overall result is higher absolute returns for one additional grade of schooling for men than for women (that is, 48 versus 26 additional cordobas per fortnight), despite the higher rate of return for women.

Household Productivity. Schooling can have a number of important productivity effects besides those reflected in the labor market. Many of these effects can occur in household production of socioeconomic outcomes like health and nutrition, which in turn can affect the schooling success of children and the labor market productivity and earnings of adults. More schooling can increase household productivity because more-schooled individuals know a wider or better set of procedures for food and water preparation, disease prevention and care, and so forth, or because they are more efficient in implementing given procedures. For example, more-schooled individuals can be more likely to know practices for preventing dysentery, more efficient in implementing such practices, or both. Because women dominate household production in most societies, including Latin American societies (Engle, 1980), we focus on the role of female schooling in household productivity.

Our estimates indicate considerable direct effects of women's schooling on child health and nutrition, child mortality, and average household nutrition (Table 1, rows 4-6). Generally, these effects are both fairly substantial and more important than those of general income improvements. In regard to nutrition, this pattern of results contrasts with the relative emphasis of the World Bank (1980), Ward and Sanders (1980), and others on the key role of income improvements, as opposed to the role of education. We find women's schooling to be more important than generalized income improvements, apparently because increased expenditures on food with rising income reflect changes primarily in food composition and increased purchase of processed food, not improvements in nutrients. However, we do not find evidence of an important direct role of women's schooling on adult health (Wolfe and Behrman, 1982a).

Generally, it is difficult to determine whether the association between household productivity and women's schooling means that the more schooled are more informed or that they are more efficient. We also are not able to identify the relative importance of these two factors. But, our estimates in row 7 of Table 1 regarding knowledge of modern contraceptives indicate that the contribution of schooling to the increased probability of knowing options is a significant factor in some cases. In this example, an additional year of schooling for a woman in the rural region with otherwise average characteristics increases the probability of knowledge by 19 percent—a fairly substantial effect.

As we have just noted, increased schooling can increase market productivity indirectly by such means as improving the health and nutrition of household members who participate in the production of market goods. Leibenstein (1957), for example, has suggested that such effects can be considerable in developing countries due to widespread nutritional and health deficiencies. We find some support for such a role for nutrition in our estimates of the earnings functions discussed here in regard to the impact of one's own schooling on labor market outcomes. Perhaps the strongest evidence for such an effect comes from the role of women's schooling in the determination of men's earnings, even after the impact of men's schooling has been accounted for.

The estimates in row 8 of Table 1 for the coefficients of women's schooling in men's earnings functions are substantial in the urban regions — not much smaller than those for men's schooling. This suggests that women's schooling may have a very substantial impact on male productivity, a possibility that is generally overlooked.

Finally, we note that generalizations to dynamic contexts from cross section household productivity effects of schooling require care, just as in the case of labor market productivity effects. For example, if there are current high household productivity gains to women's schooling because more-schooled women are much more likely to treat unsafe water correctly, as the World Bank (1980) claims is the case in Sri Lanka, these gains may be eliminated over time if safe water is provided. But, while the general point that dynamic generalizations for household as well as market productivity must be made with care, the details can differ significantly. As long as certain functions related to health, nutrition, and so forth are basically fulfilled within the household, the household productivity effects of schooling are relatively independent of schooling levels in other households. This independence contrasts with the interdependences of market productivities and implies that the cross section estimates for the impact of schooling on household productivities generalize to the effects of dynamic aggregate changes in schooling, much more than they do in the case of market productivities.

Other Impacts of Schooling on Individual Socioeconomic Outcomes. Of course, there are a large number of other possible socioeconomic impacts of schooling. We have been able to explore a few of these, including possible impacts on fertility and contraceptive use, probability of having a mate, assortive mating (for example, a more-schooled woman marries a more-schooled man), and migration. Our estimates generally suggest a significant direct positive association between women's schooling and fertility (except in urban areas other than the central metropolis), use of modern contraceptives, schooling of her mate, and migration (except for those few who originated in the other urban regions). For the probability of having a male companion, the relation with schooling is negative at younger ages but positive at older ones, with the two effects about balancing out over the life cycle (Behrman and Wolfe, 1982f). We interpret this pattern as indicating that more-schooled women are less likely to have male companions while younger because they are in school or engaged in some form of subsequent self-development, but that they are more likely to have male companions when older because they fare better in the marriage market.

In addition to these direct effects, of course, there are some important indirect effects. For example, if the indirect effects of schooling through the woman's predicted labor market earnings are added to the direct positive effects, the total impact on fertility is negative for the urban regions (Behrman and Wolfe, 1982a). Of course, this inverse association between women's schooling and fertility is a standard result. However, there is an advantage to our decomposition of this effect between that due to labor market options and that due to other causes. Some changes other than schooling can alter labor market options (for example, changed foreign or domestic demand, changed sexual discrimination against women), but this impact may be unclear if the multiple effects of schooling are mixed together, as they are in other estimates. In our case, for illustration, the impact of labor market improvements would be underestimated if their effects were mixed with the direct effect of opposite sign, as in the conventional procedure.

Similarly, schooling affects the probabilities of migrating in important but indirect ways. The probability of moving from a given origin to a given destination depends upon comparisons of expected outcomes in both and in other alternatives. Traditionally, analyses of migration have focused on comparisons of expected wages or earnings (Harris and Todaro, 1970), which in our case imply strong migratory incentives at the margin for the more schooled to move from rural to urban regions (Table 1, rows 2 and 3). But, migratory patterns cannot be explained simply as a response to expected wages or earnings, since there are many cross-flows, with both quantum movements between the rural and central metropolitan regions and step movements through the intermediate other urban regions. Elsewhere (Behrman and Wolfe, 1982c), we present evidence that micromigratory patterns for women also respond significantly to the differential regional probabilities of labor force participation, to "demographic marriage market" concerns relating to the probabilities of finding a companion (Thadani and Todaro, 1979), and to "economic marriage market" concerns relating to companion's expected earnings (Behrman and Wolfe, 1982f), as well as to expected wages and earnings. Nevertheless, the single most important determinant of the expected labor market and marriage market outcomes in various geographical regions is one's schooling. Thus, schooling has pervasive and important indirect effects on migration, in addition to the direct effects included in Table 1.

Income Distribution. The World Bank (1980) has emphasized the great potential in using the distribution of schooling to help to attain more equal income distributions and to improve the relative position of the poorest. The significant and fairly substantial impact of schooling on earnings displayed in rows 2 and 3 of Table 1 suggest that such a policy can be effective, since earnings account for the majority of household incomes.

Behrman, Wolfe, and Blau (1981) investigate the impact of hypothetical schooling (and other) policies on the distribution of household income using simulations based on estimated relations for earnings and other income components. These authors consider such policies as adding two years of schooling for all men and women, raising rural schooling levels to the urban average by adding equal increments for all rural residents, and raising women's schooling to men's averages by adding equal increments to all women. Their simulations indicate some induced progressive redistribution as a result of each of these policies, particularly the second, which is directed toward rural areas. But, the impact often is mixed, without necessarily either improving the shares of the poorest or reducing overall inequality in all regions. Moreover, policies targeted toward relatively low-schooled groups (for example, women) do not necessarily have progressive results, because such individuals are associated with households at all income levels. We conclude that schooling policies can play a significant role in the pursuit of income distribution goals. But, fairly general policies are not likely to have very progressive effects. Instead, progressive results are likely to be attained only by policies directed toward those with low income (for example, rural residents), who are not necessarily those with low schooling.

Improved Efficiency Versus Changed Tastes. Most economists interpret the estimated impact of schooling on socioeconomic outcomes as reflecting efficiency improvements, while tastes (preferences) remain constant. However, some economists—and many noneconomists—suggest that changes in taste can be induced by schooling. Whether changes in taste do occur makes an important difference in interpreting the welfare implications of schooling, as we discuss later in this chapter. Most often, however, it is difficult to know whether such changes are indeed occurring.

We think, however, that our estimated significant direct impact of schooling on household productivity and on other outcomes probably reflects in part induced changes in taste. We argue that this is the case because we also include women's productivity in market activities in these estimates and because we believe that many dimensions of market and nonmarket productivities are highly correlated. If so, the often significant direct schooling effects partially represent nonefficiency concerns above and beyond the productivity effects, and we think that tastes are the leading candidate. This argument is indirect, but if it is valid, the impact of schooling is more ambiguous in private welfare implications (that is, on personal well-being) than most economists and many others often suggest. Moreover, the argument already noted above—that the dynamic impact of schooling diminishes as relatively high-schooled individuals become less scarce—loses some of its force (or, at least, changes its character) if schooling not only represents the value of time in market alternatives but also, in part, changes tastes.

Welfare Implications. The welfare implications of the impact of schooling may be more ambiguous than it is often assumed. First, as already noted in regard to row 1 of Table 1, one significant impact of schooling seems to be that it increases the labor force participation of women in activities involving the production of market goods and services. This tends to raise market production of goods and services and thus to increase measured economic growth. But, such a shift can also result in lowered household productivity or in reduced leisure, both of which have welfare effects, but neither of which is captured very well in conventional statistical measures of socioeconomic outcomes. Because of their failure to capture such reductions in nonmarket activity, standard measures tend to overstate the positive productivity of schooling.

Second, to the extent that schooling affects tastes, the private welfare effects are much more ambiguous than they are usually recognized to be. For example, consider the widespread inverse association found between female schooling and fertility. To the extent that this reflects individual choice as a result of better information or increased efficiency in using contraceptives (which, we have already argued, is part of the impact of schooling), the reduced fertility undoubtedly increases the private welfare of current adults. But, to the extent that schooling produces changes in tastes that result in preference for consumption of goods and services and leisure over having large numbers of children, the private welfare effects are ambiguous, precisely because of the changed tastes. It is very difficult to know what better off and worse off mean if the comparison is between two situations in which tastes are different. The reductions in fertility may have clear social gains as a result of the reduction in congestion and the drop in social use of resources to educate children, but it is very difficult to know whether there are also private gains.

Third, more generally, whether one takes a private or a social viewpoint can create discrepancies in the productivity of schooling. A vivid example is provided by the estimated labor market returns in rows 3, 4, and 8 of Table 1. If they do indeed reflect on true productivity gains, they indicate, taken in conjunction with the assortive mating on schooling implied in row 1, that, for a woman with average characteristics, the productivity in terms of market goods and services of an additional grade of schooling is her own added market productivity plus the added market productivity induced in her companion by her added household productivity (that is, 26 + 38 = 64 cordobas per fortnight). From the private point of view of the woman (or of her parents), the expected return from her schooling for her expected adult household income is much larger. With one more year of her own schooling, her spouse is expected to have .68 more grades of schooling (row 11), so the woman's expected adult household income increases by an additional 33 cordobas per fortnight (that is, .68 × 48 cordobas per fortnight from row 3). However, the marriage market return, while very real and important from the point of view of the woman, does not reflect a social gain, since it is merely a redistribution of male companions with associated schooling levels and related productivities among women.

Family Background, Sibling Data, and Impact of Schooling

The empirical estimates that we have been discussing are based on analysis of adult socioeconomic outcomes of individuals or their adult households, as are all other available estimates of the socioeconomic impact of schooling in developing countries and almost all such estimates for industrialized countries. But, such estimates can be biased if important, unobserved characteristics are associated with grades of schooling completed. Important examples of such characteristics include genetic endowments and family environment, emphasized for industrial countries by Behrman and others (1980), and quality of schools, emphasized by Summers and Wolfe (1977) for the United States and by Behrman and Birdsall (1982) for Latin American nations.

For developing countries, we have the unique possibility of using sibling data to control for family-related background in explaining the role of schooling in the determination of adult socioeconomic outcomes. In collecting our data for Nicaragua, we interviewed a subsample of adult sisters of the original respondents. Elsewhere (Behrman and Wolfe, 1982d), we have used these sibling data to obtain estimates of the determinants of schooling, adult socioeconomic status, adult household income, and adult health. In each case, we include individual estimates, in which the members of this subsample are treated as individuals as in standard procedures; family average estimates, in which all observations are the average among sisters within a family, which enables us to estimate between-family effects; and deviation estimates, in which each observation is the deviation of each individual from her family average, which permits us to characterize within-family effects after controlling completely for common elements of family-related background. These estimates lead to the following important insights regarding the productivity of schooling for our developing country sample.

Role of Family Background in Determining Schooling. About two thirds of the variation in individual schooling in this subsample is due to observed and unobserved family-related effects. This suggests a stronger role of family background in determining schooling for this population than similar estimates do for the United States.

Among the observed family background variables, the most important in directly determining schooling and in indirectly determining adult outcomes are the schooling levels of the parents. That of the mother is significantly more important than that of the father. This intergenerational impact may be another element of school productivity that is often overlooked. But, whether it is overlooked or not depends on what parental schooling represents.

Father's schooling might represent his wealth or earnings, his genetic endowments, or his tastes for schooling (perhaps as transmitted by his role model). It is unlikely to represent efficiency in household production, including home education of children, since males spend so little time in such activities (Engle, 1980). That father's schooling has an equally strong effect between half-siblings who have different fathers but who were raised in the same household as between families suggests that father's schooling may in substantial part represent genetic endowments regarding capabilities and preferences. To the extent that father's schooling is a proxy for genetic endowments, of course, it would be wrong to attribute the significant coefficient estimate of his schooling to school productivity.

In comparison with father's schooling, mother's schooling might equally well represent genetic endowments; it is probably more related to household tastes regarding child raising, because of the primacy of women in such matters (Engle, 1980); and it is less likely to reflect household income or wealth, because of the much smaller contribution of women in this regard (Wolfe, Behrman, and Blau, 1982). Since the coefficient estimate for mother's schooling is significantly larger than it is for father's, this provides further evidence that genetic endowments are more important than household income. The difference also suggests that increased productivity in raising children and changes in tastes have a substantial role. Unfortunately, we cannot separate taste from efficiency effects here for the current generation of respondents as we have done earlier because we do not have information on the labor market options of the previous generation. To the extent that mother's schooling improves efficiency in household production, of course, schooling has a true intergenerational impact on productivity.

Biases in Standard Estimates of the Impact of Schooling. The previous paragraph and the preceding discussion have indicated a number of ways in which standard estimates of the impact of schooling on socioeconomic outcomes can be biased because schooling serves as a proxy for unobserved variables. Many of the generally unobserved variables related to ability and motivation are associated with family-related background, including genetic endowment, home environment, and schooling quality. If such factors cause important biases, the estimated intrafamily impact of schooling probably differs substantially from the interfamily or individual estimates. Our estimates suggest that the upward bias in standard estimates of the impact of schooling on productivity of goods and services and on income resulting from failure to control for family-related background can be considerable; indeed, the standard procedure gives estimates on the order of magnitude of twice the true values. Thus, standard estimates can substantially overstate the market productivity returns from investment in schooling in the developing countries. Nevertheless, even after correcting for such bias, the private incentives for investment in schooling can be considerable if marriage market considerations are incorporated into the analyses; for example, for women with average characteristics, we obtain an estimated rate of return of 33 percent for their expected adult household income.

Concluding Remarks

The effect of schooling, particularly for women, appears to be pervasive in developing countries, as exemplified in the case under study here. But, the interpretation of these effects can be difficult. Aggregate estimates can be misleading as a result of substantial regional and sectoral differentials. True schooling productivity can be overstated if several influential factors are overlooked. Such factors include the costs of induced reductions in nonmarket activities; the extent to which schooling serves as a proxy for unobserved family environments, genetic endowments, and school quality; and the possibly substantial impact on tastes, which creates considerable ambiguity in regard to private welfare effects. True schooling productivity can also be understated if the impact of nonmarket outcomes, which may have an important intergenerational dimension through household productivity in raising children, and marriage market considerations are not taken into account.

Our estimates indicate that such biases in standard estimates of school productivity in developing countries are sometimes very large indeed. These biases can cause considerable distortions in understanding the private and social incentives for investment in schooling and the true productivities of such investments.

Comparing our estimates with the standard interpretations, we note that the impacts of schooling on social productivity as measured by market goods and services are often overstated as a result of biases created by the omission of ability and motivation variables related to family background. Likewise, the impact of schooling on fertility and on a number of other important socioeconomic outcomes can be misunderstood as a result of the failure to recognize induced changes in taste, which have ambiguous implications for private welfare. In contrast, the possibly important effects on household productivity, such as those related to nutrition, are often overlooked. Moreover, that private returns can substantially exceed social returns as a result of marriage market considerations is generally ignored.

Thus, the productivity of schooling in developing countries probably often is considerable, but the distortions in understanding the impact of alternative educational policies created by biases in the standard procedures and interpretations of school productivity in the developing economies can be considerable — and seriously misleading.

References

Behrman, J. R., and Birdsall, N. *Income Returns to Quantity and Quality of Schooling in Brazil: Is Quantity Alone Misleading?* Washington, D.C.: World Bank, 1982.

Behrman, J. R., and others. *Socioeconomic Success: A Study of the Effects of Genetic Endowments, Family Environment, and Schooling.* Amsterdam: North-Holland, 1980.

Behrman, J. R., and Wolfe, B. L. *Earnings and Labor Force Participation in a Developing Country: Are There Sexual Differentials?* Philadelphia: University of Pennsylvania, 1981a.

Behrman, J. R., and Wolfe, B. L. *Sectoral and Geographical Labor Market Segmentation and Earnings Functions in a Developing Country.* Philadelphia: University of Pennsylvania, 1981b.

Behrman, J. R., and Wolfe, B. L. *Fertility Determinants in a Developing Country: Is the Standard Approach Too Simple and Possibly Misleading?* Philadelphia: University of Pennsylvania, 1982a.

Behrman, J. R., and Wolfe, B. L. *Knowledge and Use of Modern Contraceptives in a Developing Country: Are the Effects of Women's Schooling Often Misunderstood?* Philadelphia: University of Pennsylvania, 1982b.

Behrman, J. R., and Wolfe, B. L. *Micro Determinants of Female Migration in a Developing Country: Are Labor Market or Marriage Market Considerations More Important?* Philadelphia: University of Pennsylvania, 1982c.

Behrman, J. R., and Wolfe, B. L. *More Evidence on Nutrition Demand: Still Income Seems Overrated and Women's Schooling Underemphasized.* Philadelphia: University of Pennsylvania, 1982d.

Behrman, J. R., and Wolfe, B. L. *The Socioeconomic Impact of Schooling in a Developing Country: Is Family Background Critical? Are There Biases Due to Omitted Family Background Controls?* Philadelphia: University of Pennsylvania, 1982e.

Behrman, J. R., and Wolfe, B. L. *Who Marries Whom? And How It Affects the Returns to Schooling.* Philadelphia: University of Pennsylvania, 1982f.

Behrman, J. R., and Wolfe, B. L. "Women's Labor Force Participation and Earnings Determinants in a Developing Country." In *Proceedings of International Economic Association Sixth World Congress, Mexico City, 1980.* 1982g.

Behrman, J. R., Wolfe, B. L., and Blau, D. M. *Human Capital and Income Distribution in a Developing Country.* Discussion Paper 65–81. Madison: University of Wisconsin, 1981.

Behrman, J. R., Wolfe, B. L., and Tunali, F. I. *Determinants of Women's Earnings in a Developing Country: A Double Selectivity, Extended Human Capital Approach.* Discussion Paper 59–80. Madison: Institute for Research on Poverty, University of Wisconsin, 1981.

Engle, P. L. *The Intersecting Needs of Working Women and Their Young Children: A Report to the Ford Foundation.* San Luis Obispo, Calif.: California Polytechnical State University, 1980.

Harris, J. R., and Todaro, M. P. "Migration, Unemployment, and Development: A Two-Sector Analysis." *American Economic Review,* 1970, *60,* 126–142.

Leibenstein, H. *Economic Backwardness and Economic Growth.* New York: McGraw-Hill, 1957.

Summers, A. A. and Wolfe, B. L. "Do Schools Make a Difference? *American Economic Review,* 1977, *67* (4), 639–658.

Thadani, V. N., and Todaro, M. P. *Female Migration in Developing Countries: A Framework for Analysis.* Working Paper No. 47. New York: Population Council, Center for Policy Studies, 1979.

Tobin. J. "Comment." *Journal of Political Economy,* 1973, *81* (2, Part II), S275–S278.

Ward, J. O., and Sanders, J. H. "Nutritional Determinants and Migration in the Brazilian Northeast: A Case Study of Rural and Urban Ceara." *Economic Development and Cultural Change,* 1980, *29,* 141–163.

Wolfe, B. L. and Behrman, J. R. *Determinants of Adult Women's Health Status in a Developing Country.* Philadelphia: University of Pennsylvania, 1982a.

Wolfe, B. L., and Behrman, J. R. "Determinants of Child Mortality, Health and Nutrition in a Developing Country." *Journal of Development Economics,* 1982b.

Wolfe, B. L., and Behrman, J. R. "Is Income Overrated in Determining Adequate Nutrition?" *Economic Development and Cultural Change,* 1982c.

Wolfe, B. L., Behrman, J. R., and Blau, D. "The Impact of Demographic Changes on Income Distribution in a Developing Country." *Journal of Development Economics,* 1982, *2,* 1–31.

World Bank. *World Development Report, 1980.* Washington, D.C.: World Bank, 1980.

World Bank. *World Development Report, 1981.* Washington, D.C.: World Bank, 1981.

Barbara L. Wolfe is associate professor of economics and of preventative medicine and research associate of the Institute for Research on Poverty at the University of Wisconsin, Madison.

Jere R. Behrman is professor of economics and associate of the Population Studies Center of the University of Pennsylvania and Academic Visitor at ICERD of the London School of Economics and Political Science.

*A "second best" approach — reintroducing educational productivity
analyses into school finance reform strategies — may help to promote
efficiency in the provision of educational services.*

The Budget Crunch:
Educational Production
Functions as a Resource
Allocation Tool

Stephen Mullin

The primary purpose of this chapter is to suggest an approach to school finance reform strategy for the 1980s, an approach designed to adapt to present
political and economic constraints and to advances in our understanding of the
complex nature of the educational process. The objective is to encourage important public sector resource allocation decisions to be made rationally, not
in the haphazard fashion that usually accompanies tight budgets and sweeping
funding cuts. The proposed approach stresses efficiency in production, a concern curiously absent from most contemporary reform efforts. To this end, the
education production function framework is re-examined: Its strengths and
weaknesses as a practical policy tool are re-evaluated, and its applicability as a
"second best" solution to present reform strategies is studied. This re-examina-
tion suggests that the main role of education production functions is evalua-
tive. Through systematic analysis of input productivity and costs, these functions provide us with a means of evaluating and promoting cost-effective-

A. Summers (Ed.). *New Directions for Testing and Measurement: Productivity Assessment in Education*, no. 15.
San Francisco: Jossey-Bass, September 1982.

ness—economic efficiency—in the provision of public education. The importance of education as a public service underscores the need for promoting efficiency in the face of declining resources.

We often overlook the fact that the provision of public education is fundamentally a resource allocation issue and that, as such, it is subject to many of the same constraints that determine the levels of all publicly provided services. School finance reform has enjoyed moderate success in the past without truly assessing the resource allocation problem, at least the issue of binding budget constraints. With the current economic outlook and a shrinking public sector, traditional approaches to school finance reform are not likely to be successful in achieving new victories, or even in sustaining past reforms. In this harsh, new environment, success will require more efficient service provision—more output for less input. Although education production analyses are far from perfect, they represent the best means available for aiding policy makers in the difficult resource allocation decisions that we now face.

The chapter begins with a brief description of current school finance reform strategies, which suggests that their development was shaped by the courts, by political and economic conditions, and by the limits of our understanding of the educational process. Changes in the reform environment are then detailed, together with the likely implications for reform strategy. Possible reasons why present reformers have not responded to these changes are offered. Next, a new focus for reform is developed; it concentrates on the role of productivity measurement in efficiency as well as equity considerations. How this new approach may be implemented in Connecticut and Maryland reform movements is the subject of the following section. Finally, tentative conclusions are drawn, and suggestions for further study are offered.

The Development of Current Reform Strategy

The main thrust of reform strategy today—elimination of noneducational factors that cause expenditure disparities—is the product of three interrelated influences: a favorable political and economic climate, court rulings in legal challenges of existing state finance systems, and a belief that our knowledge of the education production process was too limited to have practical applications to school finance. In this section, these influences are reviewed, and the resulting reform strategy is summarized.

Political and Economic Conditions. During the past two decades, reform advocates clearly benefited from an environment amenable to change. Political and social concern for equity and equal opportunity assured high priority for reform efforts, and a generally upbeat economy facilitated reform measures that effectively enlarged the size of the public sector.

A basic aim of reformers was to narrow expenditure disparities that resulted from a wealth-neutral school finance structure. In practical terms, this meant expenditure equalization, and two distinct notions of how that equalization should occur developed. The most popular was a leveling-up strategy, in which wealthy districts were free to continue high spending levels, and the state would assure that poorer districts had the ability to spend as much. This approach recognized the political difficulty involved in requiring some jurisdictions to reduce spending on education; indeed, hold-harmless and grandfather legislation often precluded reduction of state aid to wealthy districts. The second equalizing approach is commonly referred to as "recapture" (Kirst, 1979, p. 428). It requires wealthy districts to pay a portion of their property tax revenues (above some tax rate level) to the state for distribution to property-poorer towns. This approach, certain to slow the growth of expenditures relative to leveling up, has been largely unsuccessful, and recapture provisions are found in only four states today (Odden, 1978). It is not difficult to see that the relative attractiveness of the leveling-up strategy over that of recapture depends on fiscal conditions that allow continual increases in expenditures, with no constraints forcing unpopular trade-offs. Almost without exceptions, the resulting reforms have led to increased aggregate expenditures on public education.

Judicial Influence. Decisions handed down in early reform cases established a precedent for judicial review of school finance systems. Early rulings rejected plaintiffs' arguments for guarantees of equal outcomes for students. The courts' general inability (and, hence, reluctance) to deal with questions of educational productivity, school inputs, and outputs (achievement outcomes, for example) significantly influenced subsequent legal reform strategies. Equal educational opportunity, a complex concept that proved difficult to define, was translated into the simple notion that educational expenditures should not be a function of a school district's property tax base. This interpretation, in a slightly expanded form, underlies most legislative responses, and it remains the basic thrust of reformers' legal approaches today.

Many courts soon recognized the limitations of the wealth-neutrality argument in reducing expenditure variations and began to deal with the many other factors that determine school spending levels. Student needs (including special and compensatory education), cost-of-education differences, municipal overburden, and local tax effort, as well as tax bases, were all identified as causes of variations in per-pupil expenditures. Of these, only variations in student needs have been considered legitimate reasons for expenditure disparities. The others have been held as evidence of unequal educational opportunity.

Limited Understanding of Education Production. The earliest legal challenges to school finance schemes argued that the uneven distribution of educational resources across districts resulted in wide variations in student outcomes. Courts rejected this approach, citing the unresolved debate over input effectiveness—popularly referred to as the "Do Schools Matter?" controversy. Basically, the courts could not rely on any established link between school inputs and outputs. Consequently, they focused on the inputs themselves, relating input availability to equality of opportunity.

At the time, academic interest in education production analysis was considerable, but interest soon diminished as its limitations were carefully delineated. Policy makers, reformers, researchers, and even the courts concluded (incorrectly, I believe) that such analyses could not be applied to finance reform. The continued success of the reform movement created little pressure to re-examine this conclusion.

The 1980s: A Different Environment

The 1970s marked a steady professionalization of state school finance reform movements. By the end of the decade, most had matured into skillfully managed and politically adept organizations, successful at building powerful coalitions, coordinating influential interest lobbies, and utilizing the expert technical capabilities of new educational policy research institutions (Berke, 1976; Fuhrman, 1979; Odden and others, 1979). Unfortunately, this newly developed ability for fine-tuning may have gone too far in shifting the focus of reform from the goals, which were never really clearly delineated, to the political and judicial means for restructuring existing systems.

As a result, today's reform cases and strategies are exceedingly complex. Legal issues are blended with a desire to mitigate the impact of any factor that can cause educational expenditures to vary beyond that amount legitimately related to student needs—reflecting reformers' preoccupation with equity concerns to the exclusion of efficiency considerations. This primary focus on equity is, in turn, a direct consequence of the climate described earlier. In many important respects, however, the climate in which school, as well as all public, services are provided today is very different from that of the late 1960s and 1970s. Although specific changes are numerous and varied, they roughly fit into the three broad categories just described: shifts in political, economic, and demographic conditions; the new judicial focus on efficiency; and advances in our ability to measure and understand complex educational issues.

Political and Economic Changes. Today's environment is particularly hostile to the reform movement. Cuts in federal aid to education, threats to the existence of the Department of Education, and an increasing willingness to provide public subsidies to private education all serve to highlight the shift in responsibility for education back to the states and localities. Further, the so-called New Federalism strengthens the notion of local control over spending and input decisions, a particular problem for reform advocates who seek greater equalization across school districts.

Unfortunately, many state and local governments are ill equipped to accept the burden of responsibility, since they face harsh fiscal pressures that severely constrain their ability to provide a full complement of public services. Further, there is growing evidence of public and political resistance to the perceived practice of solving educational problems by "throwing money at schools" (Hanushek, 1981; Kirst, 1979; Mullin and Summers, 1982). Public opposition to expenditure-increasing reform has been reinforced by statistics that show decline both in public school enrollments and in academic performance, even as per-pupil expenditures have been rising.

As a consequence of these factors, it seems unlikely that reformers can accomplish the sweeping, open-ended successes of the past. In fact, it is by no means certain that earlier gains can be sustained in today's fiscal and political environment. Several states have enacted equalization legislation, but they have been unable or unwilling to fund the new programs fully, and in some states courts and legislatures have actually reversed reform measures.

Judicial Concern with Efficiency. Although several courts have based school finance reform decisions on "thorough and efficient" clauses in their state constitutions, these clauses have typically been interpreted as requiring an equitable distribution of educational inputs. In a decision that may set a precedent for future reform cases, a Maryland court (*Somerset County Board of Education* v. *Hornbeck, et al.,* 1981) recently adopted an unusually narrow interpretation of the "thorough and efficient" requirement. In its decision, the court defined *efficient* as "using the least wasteful means." Although the court requires equal per-pupil expenditures, the important and novel point is that these funds must be spent in an efficient manner. Consequently, the court specifically rejected the case for taxpayer equity, a central theme of current reform strategy. Instead, its focus is on the student: Equal and efficient expenditures are required, regardless of how the revenues are raised. If this case does prove to be precedent setting, current reform strategy will have to include economic efficiency considerations. The burden of developing the new approach will rest primarily on reformers.

How Much Do We Know? Factors relating to our ability to identify and measure educational inputs and outputs further suggest that traditional reform strategies have become obsolete. Essentially, the state of the art has improved. After nearly two decades of experience, we are now better able to measure and value educational goals. Further, our ability to analyze the educational process itself has increased dramatically. With this greater knowledge comes closer scrutiny of the finance reform movement. Already, some debate has arisen over the movement's failure to define clear objectives of reform, while the success of past reform-motivated changes continues to be questioned (Friedman and Wiseman, 1978; Jones, 1980; Phelps and Addonizio, 1981).

One area in which theory has advanced significantly since the early years of reform is educational production analysis. Hanushek (1979) carefully documents the advances in educational production theory and its empirical applications. His review reports — as do others' (Hanushek, 1981; Madaus and others, 1980; Mullin and Summers, 1982) — surprisingly robust findings over studies that vary greatly in scope and quality. For instance, school differences consistently affect student achievement (although the direction and magnitudes of these effects vary significantly), school resources appear to "interact importantly with the background characteristics of individuals," and "there is quite conclusive evidence that schools are economically inefficient" (Hanushek, 1979, pp. 377–378).

Curiously, the substance of these analyses and their implications for efficient service provision have not been incorporated into the mainstream of school finance reform, in spite of their obvious importance. Meanwhile, courts and state legislatures are becoming increasingly proficient in these technical matters, and state legislatures face increasing fiscal pressure to get more for public expenditures.

Present Barriers to Reform. If the changed environment suggests that reform must be restructured, why have we seen so few efforts to do so? There are several possible explanations: First, reformers gain if past trends continue; that is, education funding increases. Further, the individual groups that comprise the reform coalitions lose if reform dollars are allocated with efficiency strings attached. This scenario suggests that reformers do not consider that tighter fiscal constraints are binding on the educational sector. Second, special-interest groups place a higher value on their own sectors than society as a whole does. Consequently, some reformers believe that the education output is seriously undervalued in our society today and that we are already gaining benefits far in excess of costs (Psacharopoulos, 1980). Serious efficiency incentives are being viewed as disguised cutbacks in our already suboptimal investment in education. Third, regardless of the true benefits, educational spending is often an emotional issue. The costs to a community or state of a long and serious battle over school spending levels may seem significant when children are the pawns. Reformers may view this as a powerful trump card that lessens the need to alter current strategy. Fourth, inertia may explain at least part of the reluctance. Years of strategy development, coalition building, and intense lobbying are not easily undone by threats of future problems. Perhaps actual implementation of large cuts in educational spending will provide a catalyst for change.

A New Focus for School Finance Reform

Traditional school finance strategies may prove increasingly unsuccessful in the 1980s, yet little has been proposed to restructure the reform approach in response to the changing environment. A hostile political and fiscal climate, coupled with recent court decisions, creates pressure for alternatives that emphasize efficiency in production as well as equity in distribution. Fortunately, the educational process is no longer a mysterious black box, and practical alternative approaches are feasible, although they may be difficult to implement.

A Return to Education Outputs. In a perfect world, providers of public education would strive for an optimal allocation of resources to the education sector and seek an equitable distribution of educational output among individuals. In our imperfect world of second and third best, public services are often allocated in ways that achieve neither efficiency nor equity goals. Consequently, allocations are not optimal, and distributions are clearly not perfectly equitable. Part of the problem with the provision of education is uncertainty in placing dollar values on its benefits or outputs. But, one significant reason why school finance reformers have not been truly successful in assuring optimal allocations and fair distributions is that they attempt to cover a wide range of tangential issues, including taxpayer equity, municipal overburden, and public sector employment (that is, teachers). While these objectives are certainly worthwhile, their proper place in school finance reform is not clear.

The unique position of the education sector in our society can be attributed to its output. The other considerations are related to the inputs and have no special value per se, accruing instead from their inclusion in this sector. Therefore, to address the aims and methods of school finance reform properly, primary consideration must be given to the sector's output. Judicial decisions implicitly—and explicitly in recent decisions in Ohio, New Jersey, and Maryland—support this notion by placing the focus on students. Reformers, however, embrace a politically attractive combination. They recognize that these tangential issues not only influence educational output but tap several other reform constituencies as well. A stronger case is made for increased state funding and decreased local control over school expenditure decisions. With the visible link between school taxes and school spending blurred, local "no" votes are less likely to constrain growing expenditures.

Nevertheless, legitimate differences exist in the identification and measurement of educational output. Literacy, ability to function as an adult, citizenship, character, morals, and increased productivity are among the outcomes often identified that preclude easy measurement. Academic achievement, job skills, and college admissions are among the outcomes that can be measured, albeit imprecisely. The measurement of educational outcomes is quite distinct from the values placed upon them. Since conceptual and empirical estimation of the benefits of education depends upon both measurement and evaluation, it is no wonder that there is little consensus on the level of educational provision. This holds particularly true when additional spending on education must be weighed against reductions in expenditures on other public services.

Educational Production Functions: Limitations. Clearly, allocation of resources to the public sector would be simpler if outputs could be delivered to individuals directly. However, as in most services, the public sector provides inputs, which are transformed into educational outputs in a complex production process. Demand for these inputs, therefore, is derived; the inputs themselves have no intrinsic value as educational inputs. Consequently, one key to dealing with the resource allocation issue lies in understanding this transformation or production process. Models that describe the process in measurable terms are known as educational production functions.

The conceptual and statistical problems inherent in empirical estimation of educational production functions are well known; they have been carefully discussed by Hanushek (1979) and Lau (1978). My focus here is on how production function analyses can be used in reform efforts. For such efforts, the main problems are related to data insufficiency, not to conceptual shortcomings. First, as already noted, many outputs cannot be measured. To the extent that they are valued, we have no way of estimating the production relationship. Omitting them from studies may cause the derived value of inputs or resources to be understated. Further, the observed behavior of schools (in the data collected on inputs and achievement outcomes) does not actually define a purely technical relationship between inputs and outputs, since the measured outputs also reflect school district preferences (Hanushek, 1979). Multiple outputs themselves, especially where causality is in more than one direction, pose additional estimation problems, which can be dealt with statistically (Boardman and others, 1973). Finally, observed relationships between inputs and outputs are unlikely to reflect technologically efficient production (the maximum output for any given combination of inputs); for this reason, the resulting analyses "may not be particularly useful in predicting how changes in inputs would affect outputs" (Hanushek, 1979, p. 369).

Educational Production Functions: Potential Role. While these problems impede our ability to predict exact production relationships, they do not render analysts incapable of examining the economic efficiency of the educational process. Indeed, many early applications of production function analysis concentrated on determining technical efficiency or input effectiveness. However, analyses of economic efficiency or of its less restrictive counterpart, cost-effectiveness, were notably missing from many of these studies.

Hanushek (1979, p. 376) suggests that the primary contribution of production function analysis is the identification of "independent influences of various factors...on performance of the schooling system." In other words, we can identify input productivity, at least in terms of the particular output being measured. While the impact of any given input on output will depend upon the transformation process (for example, on school organization or classroom procedures), carefully executed studies can account for this. In fact, recent research has focused on the output effect of various transformation processes.

Such studies attempt to measure the technical efficiency of schools. They estimate what they call the *educational significance* or *achievement effectiveness* of inputs, resources, or programs. Results (for example, regression coefficients) are interpreted as the marginal impact of change in a particular input on the quantity or level of educational output. In many studies, significantly positive achievement effectiveness constitutes justification for providing or increasing the level of a particular input. When inputs are lumped together as expenditures, similar conclusions are drawn. For example, one study (Wendling and Cohen, 1981) of achievement in New York State public schools finds that, assuming causality, an increase of $1,000 in per-pupil expenditure will increase average per-district achievement scores by one point. The authors consider this impact adequate justification for such an increase in school expenditures. This type of analysis and similar conclusions are very common, as researchers have been trying for years to prove that "schools do matter."

However, estimates of input productivity or achievement effectiveness alone are insufficient for dealing with resource allocation and school finance reform. Since allocation and reform require trade-offs, some means of relating output to costs must be examined; for economists, this relation involves the notion of economic efficiency. A production process is economically efficient if an optimal level of outputs is produced with the least-cost combination of inputs, given input prices. Since education produces multiple outputs and involves extensive measurement problems, economic efficiency itself is rarely examined in detail (Hanushek, 1979, 1981; Mullin and Summers, 1982).

Instead, researchers and policy makers concentrate on the less restrictive concept of cost-effectiveness, which is applicable to any level of output: Is the benefit of the additional output worth the cost of the extra input? In this form, cost-effectiveness analysis is difficult to apply to education production because of the problems inherent in the valuation of benefits. Some cases pose no problem, because the magnitudes of benefits and costs are of different scale. From the New York State example just noted, one might conclude that a one-point increase in average achievement is not worth a $3 billion increase in educational expenditures. However, many cases are not so clear-cut. Nevertheless, as budget constraints become increasingly binding, greater efforts will have to be made to deal with this valuation problem, because cuts and expenditures force implicit value judgments that will not always be in the best interest of the community or society.

Educational Production Functions: Measuring Equity. School finance reform efforts have concentrated exclusively on the equity of school finance systems. Over the years, this quest for fairness in educational opportunity has been used to justify efforts for achieving both student and taxpayer equity at the input (or expenditure) level (Odden, 1979). A natural result has been that student equity was measured in terms of expenditures, despite nearly universal agreement that expenditure levels are not ideal measures of quantity or quality of educational services.

To address the equitability of public education provision to students, educational outputs should be valued. Since this is impossible in practice, reformers and educational experts should identify the outputs that society values, that can be identified and measured, and that can be influenced by educational inputs. The outputs thus identified determine the output measure in educational production analysis. Equity standards can be constructed from statewide averages of existing outputs, or they can be determined by norms derived from a public choice process. The strong argument for this approach is that it provides a structural framework for decision making, which is otherwise carried out in an ad hoc fashion.

Academic achievement is one outcome (or vector of outcomes) that, in spite of measurement problems (Mullin and Summers, 1982), meets the three criteria just stated and that has the added advantage that it is already being measured in most states at the present time. A focus on achievement outcomes also allows for inclusion of different student needs (for example, compensatory and special education) in a more exact way than the current method of dollars-per-disadvantaged-student cost increments. Other measurable outcomes could also be used for equity standards. Weights placed on the valuation of these different outputs need not be equal across either outputs or districts. That is, certain observed differences in outcome measures (accounting for student characteristics) across districts may be a function of community preferences, not of differences in production efficiency. If this approach were incorporated into school finance reform strategies, it would mean that essentially new equity standards were being measured and compared. These standards would focus on the sector's unique product — educational outcomes. This is important for efficient resource allocation, since the public ultimately demands education outputs, not inputs. But, some may argue that it is impossible to predict (or simulate) future educational outputs so as to enable policy makers to distinguish among various potential financial schemes. Several considerations suggest that this is not a serious drawback. First, the procedure can be used as an ex post facto evaluation of existing systems or past reforms. Second, it can probably be used to predict not only future outcomes but future community spending behavior as well—a widely used forecast in legislative debate over alternative finance systems. Finally, linking of equalized aid to future positive impact may prove to be an effective way of forcing school districts to increase productivity.

Educational Production Functions: Measuring Efficiency. Consistent evidence suggesting that schools are economically inefficient has led some researchers to ask why and to propose methods for redressing the problem. One popular explanation is that schools do not minimize costs because there are no market incentives, such as profit and loss. While it could be argued that some budget constaints prevent excessively inefficient behavior, there are no major incentives to promote actual efficiency.

One might expect that a more economically efficient school system would be preferred by all parties, since greater output could be produced for an equal or reduced amount of inputs. But, equal or reduced amount of inputs—translated into dollars—is exactly what school finance reformers oppose. Convincing the reform movement to include efficiency criteria in proposed finance systems would be similar to convincing hospitals to cut costs and unions to cut wages. It might also seem similar to convincing companies to forsake short-term profits, but there is a difference. A clear measure of the wisdom of the decision lies ahead—as long-term profits.

Education production function analyses to promote efficiency can be incorporated into finance equalization schemes proposed by reformers in several ways. First, the equalization of aid could be categorical, with funds targeted to specific programs of proven effectiveness. But, evidence of input effectiveness is not robust, and this policy would prevent districts from responding to local needs and choices. A second approach would link future equalizing aid with certain performance criteria, rather than tax effort, as in district power equalizing formulas. In effect, certain districts would be penalized, not for lack of effort, but for lack of results. Both solutions pose one major problem: The state may be further harming the very students whom it sought to protect with the equalizing aid.

An equalizing formula with built-in incentives to promote efficiency might be a better approach. Such a formula has recently been described (Cohn, Sweigart, and Reeves, 1980) and will no doubt be the subject of considerable research in the future. Cohn, Sweigart, and Reeves develop a goal-programming procedure that ties state aid to measurable achievement target output levels. These targets are adjusted for varying student backgrounds. The goal is to minimize deviations from attainable output per pupil rather than to equalize tax burdens or per-pupil expenditures. Reformers could present this or other incentive-equalizing alternatives to courts and legislatures, arguing that they are the only financing schemes that meet both the equity and the efficiency requirements of state constitutions. Reformers might argue further that these formulas are more likely to be funded, since control is built in: Expenditures can rise only as output rises.

The specifics of the performance targets of any given scheme will depend upon the current state financing system, local conditions, and community preferences over education outputs. A major advantage over state-controlled programs is the flexibility that this approach allows in the selection of inputs and processes. Outputs, not inputs, are regarded as the important product, and they are therefore subject to state guidelines. Rather than being penalized with decreased state aid, districts that performed below their specified target levels would be subject to stricter guidelines and receive assistance from the state to develop more effective educational programs.

An Application to Reform in Two States

Connecticut and Maryland school finance reform movements offer useful illustrations of how the approach outlined in this chapter can be applied to actual reform strategy.

Connecticut. A flurry of activity followed the state Supreme Court decision of 1977 in *Horton* v. *Meskill.* The court held that the existing finance system, which traditionally relied on local property taxes, violated the state constitution by denying student equal educational opportunity — the standard wealth-neutrality argument. The legislature responded with a guaranteed tax base (GTB) plan (Connecticut School Finance Advisory Board, 1979) that dealt with several issues in far greater detail than explicitly required by *Horton* v. *Meskill.* To date, however, the plan remains only partially funded.

The GTB plan, first enacted in 1975 and since revised, now deals extensively with student quality and achievement. The state defined clear educational goals and outlined a program of "suitable educational experiences" that must be provided to all students. A planning-implementation-evaluation (P-I-E) plan, begun in 1979, requires that each school district's average educational output be evaluated, using standardized achievement tests and other factors. Although education production functions were not included in this evaluation process, they could play an important role in measuring input effectiveness, especially if additional output measures were used, such as variance in achievement. The P-I-E emphasizes program or input effectiveness, although it does not define achievement standards. Also, no clear penalties are established for districts that fail to meet the evaluation criteria. A program remedial process promises state assistance in the development of effective school programs for districts that fail the evaluation process.

In contrast to many reform schemes, greater taxpayer equity is not a clear product of the GTB. The plan is not fully funded, and a five-year phase-in appears behind schedule, which will further delay aid equalization. Since state revenues are not collected from income taxation, it is not evident that the resulting tax burdens will be any more equitable as state dollars replace local dollars. Finally, the aid formula calls for leveling up to the wealthiest district, and certain provisions protect many wealthy districts from receiving less aid than they presently do; both these features will further dilute the equalizing impact of GTB monies.

One important problem with the GTB is its failure to address the issue of economic efficiency, a fact underscored by the aim of the formula to level up to the top and by the absence of cost-effectiveness conditions in the evaluation procedure. Strong opposition to full funding suggests that the electorate questions whether the benefits are worth the price. Worse, mandated funding caps and matching formulas practically encourage overspending, while they provide little incentive to meet achievement effectiveness criteria.

The ultimate success of the GTB may hinge on the inclusion of efficiency incentives in the equalizing formula. Enough information has already been collected from school districts to make it possible to analyze production and identify cost-effective programs. With this information, the GTB formula could be revised to reward such behavior, and the state could assist less efficient districts with program development. If necessary, costly and ineffective programs would be eliminated or modified by state order.

Maryland. The reform movement has also been very active in Maryland in recent years. A state commission published reform recommendations in 1980 (Subcommittee on Education..., 1980), one year before the remarkable decision of the Baltimore Circuit Court in *Somerset County Board of Education* v. *Hornbeck, et al.* (1981). The commission proposed a reform package structurally similar to the GTB plan, calling for increased state equalizing aid, changes in the aid formula's definition of wealth, and further study to develop a "basic educational program," a cost-of-education index, and a scheme for distributing special and vocational education aid (Subcommittee on Education..., 1980). However, this plan was found to be unconstitutional under *Somerset* v. *Hornbeck, et al.*

The court's decision seems unique in the national school finance area, and it may well set a precedent for future cases. Taxpayer equity is specifically rejected, and economic efficiency and mathematically equal per-pupil expenditures are both required. Only expenditure variations based on cost differences are allowed, and then only if "tailored with mathematical precision to a clearly demonstrated difference in cost." Drawing on evidence of input and cost-effectiveness, the court rejected claims for additional funds for some groups of students, because there was no evidence that such funds were effective. In allowing only cost-related expenditure variations, municipal overburden was implicitly accepted, and local choice over expenditure level decisions was rejected.

The Maryland decision leaves little room for the type of legislative politics that has characterized the development of most reform systems. This does not imply that there is no room for production function analysis, however. On the contrary, cost-effectiveness and achievement analyses are practically required to justify any variations in per-pupil expenditure. It is not clear whether the finance scheme envisioned by the court will lead to greater student equity in terms of educational output, since districts need only spend the equal dollars without accounting for their effectiveness. Districts that value education will tend to strive harder for achievement effectiveness, given the funding level decisions determined by the state. A useful addition to any legislative scheme designed to meet the requirements established by *Somerset* v. *Hornbeck, et al.* would be student achievement level targets, with nonpecuniary penalties for developing cost-inefficient programs and financial rewards for developing cost-efficient programs.

Conclusion

While school finance reform is becoming an increasingly complex issue, it remains basically a resource allocation problem. In today's declining public sector, approaches to securing provision of public services that were successful in the past, concentrating as they did on equity aims, are not likely to be attractive. This may be especially true for public education, a fundamental service that affects the lives of all Americans. After a decade of state reform of school finance systems, it is not clear that equal educational opportunity for students is closer to reality or that individual tax burdens for financing a larger education sector are any more equitable.

This chapter has suggested that the school finance reform movement, which itself is responsible in part for a significant increase in school expenditures, must address the issue of resource allocation and trade-offs if future equity reforms are to succeed. The present focus on educational inputs fails to consider the sector's unique product, education output, in terms of efficiency. The new focus of reform need not imply a decreased quantity of education. Rather, finance methods should be structured to encourage more output for less input. The approach outlined in this chapter concentrates on the role of the education production process itself, and methods for reform strategies that provide incentives for efficiency in the transformation of school inputs into educational outputs have been explored. Improving such incentive schemes is an important direction for future work.

Addressing one of the basic challenges facing the public education sector today, Kirst (1979, pp. 427–428) asks, "Can education compete effectively with other public services in the 1980s?" As competition for decreasing funds leads to increasingly unpleasant trade-offs, proper methods for valuing output and measuring productivity in the education sector become more essential.

References

Berke, J. S., and others. "Two Roads to School Finance Reform." *Society,* 1976, *13* (2), 67–72.

Boardman, A. E., and others. *A Simultaneous Equations Model of the Educational Process.* Pittsburgh: School of Public and Urban Affairs, Carnegie-Mellon University, 1973.

Cohn, E., Sweigart, J. R., and Reeves, G. "A New Approach to Financing Public Schools." *Journal of Education Finance,* 1980, *6* (1), 1–17.

Connecticut School Finance Advisory Board. *A Plan for Promoting Equal Educational Opportunity in Connecticut.* Hartford: State Board of Education, 1979.

Friedman, L. S., and Wiseman, M. "Understanding the Equity Consequences of School Finance Reform." *Harvard Educational Review,* 1978, *48* (2), 193–226.

Fuhrman, S. *State Education Politics: The Case of School Finance Reform.* Education Finance Center Report No. F79-12. Denver: Education Commission of the States, 1979.

Hanushek, E. A. "Conceptual and Empirical Issues in the Estimation of Educational Production Functions." *Journal of Human Resources,* 1979, *14* (3), 351–388.

Hanushek, E. A. "Throwing Money at Schools." *Journal of Policy Analysis and Management,* 1981, *1* (1), 19–41.

Jones, T. H. "Equal Educational Opportunity Revisited." *Journal of Education Finance,* 1980, *6* (4), 471–484.

Kirst, M. W. "The New Politics of State Education Finance." *Phi Delta Kappan,* 1979, *60* (6), 427–432.

Lau, L. J. "Educational Production Functions: A Summary." Paper presented at the National Institute of Education Conference, 1978.

Madaus, G. F., and others. *School Effectiveness: A Reassessment of the Evidence.* New York: McGraw-Hill, 1980.

Mullin, S. P., and Summers, A. A. *Is More Better? An Analysis of the Evidence of the Effectiveness of Spending on Compensatory Education.* Philadelphia: University of Pennsylvania, 1982.

Odden, A. *School Finance Reform in the States: 1978.* Education Finance Center Report No. F78-1. Denver: Education Commission of the States, 1978.

Odden, A., and others. *Equity in School Finance.* Education Finance Center Report No. F79-9. Denver: Education Commission of the States, 1979.

Phelps, J. L., and Addonizio, M. F. "District Power Equalizing: Cure-All or Prescription?" *Journal of Education Finance,* 1981, *7* (1), 64–87.

Psacharopoulos, G. "Spending on Education in an Era of Economic Stress: An Optimist's View." *Journal of Education Finance,* 1980, *6* (2), 160–175.

Somerset County Board of Education v. *Hornbeck, et al.* Circuit Court of Baltimore City, 119A 115 File No. A58438, 1981.

94

Subcommittee on Education of the Task Force to Study State–Local Fiscal Relationships. "Report of the Subcommittee on Education of the Task Force to Study State–Local Fiscal Relationships." Annapolis, Md.: Department of Fiscal Services, 1980.

Wendling, W., and Cohen, J. "Education Resources and Student Achievement: Good News for Schools." *Journal of Education Finance,* 1981, *7* (1), 44–63.

Stephen Mullin, a research associate with the Public Enterprise Research Program, University of Pennsylvania, has had training and experience in the fields of public, health care, and education finance.

An annotated list of further sources follows.

Sources of Additional Assistance

Anita A. Summers

Behrman, J. R., and others. *Socioeconomic Success: A Study of the Effects of Genetic Endowments, Family Environment, and Schooling.* Amsterdam: North-Holland, 1980.

    Uses twin data to control for family background in obtaining estimates of impact of schooling on earnings and occupational status in the United States. Concludes that standard procedures substantially overestimate impact of schooling because they fail to control for family background-related ability and motivation.

Behrman, J. R., and Wolfe, B. L. "The Socioeconomic Impact of Schooling in a Developing Country: Is Family Background Critical? Are There Biases Due to Omitted Family Background Controls?" Philadelphia: University of Pennsylvania, 1982.

    Uses data on adult sisters to explore determinants of schooling in a developing country. Concludes that family background, but not adult income and socioeconomic status, is more important for determining schooling in underdeveloped countries than it is in developed countries and that standard procedures substantially overestimate effects of schooling in developing countries due to failure to control for family background-related ability and motivation.

A. Summers (Ed.). *New Directions for Testing and Measurement: Productivity Assessment in Education,* no. 15.
San Francisco: Jossey-Bass, September 1982.

Birdsall, N., and Cochrane, S. H. "Education and Parental Decision Making: A Two-Generation Approach." In L. Anderson and D. Windham (Eds.), *Education and Development.* Lexington, Mass.: Lexington Press, forthcoming.

Reviews studies of determinants of schooling in developing countries as well as the consequences of schooling for family decision making with respect to fertility and child mortality.

Brown, B. W., and Saks, D. H. "The Production and Distribution of Cognitive Skills Within Schools." *Journal of Political Economy,* 1975, *83,* 571–594.

Explains that the results of school effectiveness research reflect both technical relationships between inputs and outputs and the tastes of teachers concerning the allocation of class time. Consequently, a satisfactory model of the education process must explore the determinants of teachers' time allocations.

Cohn, E., Sweigart, J. R., and Reeves, G. "A New Approach to Financing Public Schools." *Journal of Education Finance,* 1980, *6* (1), 1–17.

Develops a goal-programming (input-output) financing scheme for the distribution of state aid to promote efficient school spending. Discusses conceptual and practical problems, and presents simulated results of the impact of a plan on a typical school district.

Hanushek, E. A. "Conceptual and Empirical Issues in the Estimation of Educational Production Functions." *Journal of Human Resources,* 1979, *14* (3), 351–388.

Reviews the extensive educational production function literature, discusses a variety of technical issues, and places this literature in the context of economic research on the determinants of human capital.

Hanushek, E. A. "Throwing Money at Schools." *Journal of Policy Analysis and Management,* 1981, *1* (1), 19–41.

Reviewing the evidence on the relationship between expenditures and performance, the author concludes that there is no consistent relationship and advocates performance incentives rather than more dollars.

Jamison, D. T., and Lockheed, M. E. "Participation in Schooling: Determinants and Learning Outcomes in Nepal." World Bank Population and Human Resources Division Discussion Paper No. 81. Washington, D.C.: The World Bank, 1981.

Shows intergenerational effects of ability and schooling, but no effects of school availability, on participation in school of the current generation of children.

Kirst, M. "The New Politics of State Education Finance." *Phi Delta Kappan,* 1979, *60* (6), 427–432.

Reviews school finance reform history and suggests a restructuring of traditional reform approaches in response to today's tight budget constraints.

McDermott, J. E. (Ed.). *Indeterminacy in Education.* Berkeley, Calif.: McCutchan, 1976.

Surveys the state of the art of educational research on the relationship between cost and quality and the public policy implications for legal issues relating to school finance, desegregation, and school decentralization.

Sheffield, J. R. "Retention of Literacy and Basic Skills: A Review of the Literature." Paper prepared for the Education Department of the World Bank.

Reviews the literature on cognitive consequences of formal and nonformal education in developing countries.

Summers, A. A., and Wolfe, B. L. "Do Schools Make a Difference?" *American Economic Review,* September 1977.

Analyzes the effects of school inputs on learning, using pupil-specific analysis of Philadelphia data to show that some inputs are effective, that pupil-specific data are needed to reveal their effectiveness, and that inputs affect students differentially.

World Bank. *World Development Report, 1980.* Washington, D.C.: World Bank, 1980.

Reviews existing evidence regarding impact of schooling in developing countries, and concludes that increased schooling, particularly at the primary level, can have substantial positive effects on productivity, income distribution, fertility, health, and nutrition.

Anita A. Summers is professor and associate chairperson of public management in the Wharton School of the University of Pennsylvania.

Index

W